EURIPIDES

Medea

translated by
J. MICHAEL WALTON

with commentary and notes by
MARIANNE McDONALD, *Professor of Theatre and Classics, University of California, San Diego,* and J. MICHAEL WALTON, *Professor of Drama, University of Hull*

METHUEN DRAMA

Methuen Student Edition

10 9 8 7 6 5 4 3 2 1

This edition first published in the United Kingdom in 2002 by
Methuen Publishing Ltd
215 Vauxhall Bridge Road, London SW1V 1EJ

This translation of *Medea* first published in 2000 by Methuen
Publishing Ltd in *Euripides Plays: 1* Copyright © 2000 by J. Michael
Walton

Commentary and notes copyright © 2002 by Marianne McDonald
and J. Michael Walton

The right of the authors to be identified as the authors of these works
have been asserted by them in accordance with the Copyright,
Designs and Patents Act, 1988

Methuen Publishing Limited Reg. No. 3543167

A CIP catalogue record for this book is available from
the British Library

ISBN 0 413 77030 3

Cover photograph: Medea (Nike Imoru), Delphi, 2000. Courtesy of
the University of Hull Photographic Service

Typeset by Deltatype, Birkenhead, Wirral
Printed and bound in Great Britain by
Cox & Wyman Ltd, Reading, Berkshire

Contents

Euripides: *c.* 485/480–406 BC

c. 1200	The Trojan War.
c. 850	Composition by Homer of the epic poems *The Iliad* and *The Odyssey*.
c. 776	First Olympiad.
560–27	The tyranny of Pisistratus in Athens.
c. 550	Inauguration of the Festival of the Great Dionysia, including performance of a cyclical dance known as the dithyramb and the recitation of the Homeric poems by a bard or rhapsode.
c. 532	Invention of tragedy (attributed to Thespis, the first actor). Performances probably in the *agora*.
c. 525	Birth of Aeschylus.
510	Expulsion of Hippias, the last king of Athens. First moves towards democracy in Athens.
c. 500	Introduction of comedy in Attica and in Sicily. Performances in Athens move from the Agora to the south-east of the Acropolis. Aeschylus first presents plays and introduces a second actor. Prizes for tragedy first awarded.
c. 496	Birth of Sophocles.
490	Battle of Marathon. Athens defeats the invading Persians.
c. 486	Comic performances formalised at the Festivals of the Great Dionysia and the Lenaea. Prizes awarded.
c. 485–80	Euripides born near Athens.

480   Following the evacuation of Athens, Persians
           defeated again at the sea battle of Salamis, and by
           the Spartans the following year at Plataea.

477   Creation of the Delian League by Athens, which
           is the basis of the Athenian Empire.

472   Aeschylus' *Persians*, the first surviving Greek
           tragedy.

469   Birth of Socrates.

468   Sophocles first presents a group of plays at the
           Great Dionysia and defeats Aeschylus.

461   Reforms of Ephialtes. Powers removed from Court
           of the Areopagus. Jury system, with pay, and
           people's courts established. Ephialtes assassinated
           and Pericles becomes leader of the democratic
           party.

458   Aeschylus' *Oresteia*, dealing with the institution of
           the rule of law by jury and the setting up of the
           Areopagus.

456   Death of Aeschylus in Sicily.

455   Euripides first competes at the Great Dionysia
           with *The Daughters of Pelias* (now lost).

449   Competition for tragic actors introduced.

447–18   Building programme in Athens includes the
           Precinct of Dionysus to house the Theatre, the
           Odeon of Pericles and the Great Hall.

c. 445   Birth of Aristophanes.

441   Euripides wins his first dramatic prize (titles
           unknown).

c. 440   Sophocles' *Antigone*.

438   Euripides' *Alcestis*, his first extant play.

431   *Medea*. Beginning of Peloponnesian War between
           Athens and Sparta.

c. 430	*Children of Heracles.*
430–29	Plague in Athens. Death of Pericles.
428	*Hippolytus*, which won first prize.
427	Birth of Plato.
425	*Acharnians*, first surviving play of Aristophanes.
c. 425	*Andromache.*
c. 424	*Hecuba*; *Cyclops* (possibly in the same group as *Hecuba*).
?424–20	*Suppliant Women.*
?422–14	*Electra.*
421	Aristophanes' *Peace*. Peace of Nicias (temporary).
416	Conquest of Melos.
c. 415	*Heracles.*
415	*Trojan Women.*
415–13	Sicilian expedition followed by Athenian defeat.
c. 414	*Iphigeneia in Tauris.*
414	Aristophanes' *Birds.*
c. 413	*Ion.*
412	*Helen.*
411	Aristophanes' *Thesmophoriazousae*. Short-lived oligarchic revolution in Athens.
c. 409	*Phoenician Women.*
408	*Orestes.*
407	Euripides leaves Athens for Macedon.
406	Death of Euripides (in Macedon) and Sophocles.
405	*Iphigeneia at Aulis*, *Alcmaeon in Corinth* (now lost) and *Bacchae* performed posthumously, winning first prize.
	Aristophanes' *Frogs* featuring a competition in Hades between Aeschylus and Euripides.
404	Surrender of Athenians to the Spartans; pulling down of the Great Walls and the end of the

Plot

Because the body of myth from which the plots of the
tragedies were taken was so flexible and so fluid, each
member of the audience might come to a new play with a
different set of expectations and prejudices. Some of the more
equivocal characters, Helen, Heracles, Odysseus, could be
treated as heroes or villains, tragic or comic, according to the
fresh context which each playwright might devise. They
brought with them a certain amount of baggage, beauty,
brawn, guile, but beyond that they were new creations in the
same way as Don Juan might be in Molière, Mozart or
Frisch; or, indeed as might Medea be in Seneca, Charpentier
or Franca Rame. There is, then, a lot of information to be
looked for about both the past and the present in the
exposition to each play, that opening sequence in which the
circumstances of *this* play are laid out for the audience.

In the prologue from the Nurse in Euripides' *Medea*, we
hear of the expedition to Colchis on the *Argo* to fetch the
Golden Fleece; of Medea becoming 'besotted with her Jason';
of her escaping with him to Iolcos and persuading the
daughters of Pelias to kill their father; exile to Corinth with
Jason and their two children; Jason's recent betrayal by
agreeing to marry the daughter of the King of Corinth and
Medea's distraught reaction to the news. Subsequent scenes
offer further revelations about the past, including Medea's
claim that without her Jason would never have achieved
anything.

This information can be fed into what is known of the myth from other versions by Homer, Pindar and Apollonius Rhodius. Jason was the son of Aeson, King of Iolcos in Thessaly, whose throne was usurped by a half-brother, Pelias. Jason's subsequent upbringing and attempt to regain the kingdom involved the expedition in the *Argo* to fetch the Golden Fleece (see pages xxix–xxx below). Eventually Jason, Medea and their two children found themselves living in exile in Corinth where the action of Euripides' play takes place.

Apart from revealing some of the context of the play the Nurse also offers in the prologue two important pieces of information. Firstly, the people of Corinth are concerned for Medea. Secondly, she is regarded as having been 'a good wife' to Jason. The Nurse is worried, though, that the way she has reacted to the news will lead to disaster: 'I know her but she frightens me' (l.39). These words are followed closely by the first entry of the children, an important entrance for establishing what the play is really about. Though they do not speak until their voices are heard off-stage at the end trying to avoid their mother, the presence of the boys is a major physical pivot for the action, first here, then in the second scene with Jason where they are asked to carry the deadly gifts to the Princess (ll.895–975). Their subsequent return and Medea's farewell to them (ll.1001–77) are as moving as any scene in Greek tragedy. On the page it is easy to forget how much of an impact their physical presence makes.

Back to the opening, and the arrival of the Tutor offers another dimension, the story as seen by the only sympathetic male character, eventually to be used as part of the instrument of Medea's revenge. His departure heralds the entry of the Chorus, local women, compassionate but phlegmatic too:

Your husband's deserted you.
For someone else's bed.
That's not the end of the world. (ll.155–7)

Only after the immensely dense and concentrated first 200
lines does Medea make her appearance. All her first lines,
identifying her despair, are delivered from off-stage, so that
the apparent calmness of her opening speech to the Chorus
conveys just that sense of foreboding and alarm that the
Nurse had identified in herself. Her appeal to the women of
the Chorus as women and her engagement of their help is
crucial here and reveals a Medea whose ability to manipulate
those around her is highly honed.

When Creon arrives she tries a variety of means to buy the
time she needs, from abject pleading to reasoned argument,
before finding what does work and gaining her 'one day'.
From this point on, with the Chorus already suborned, the
plot gathers momentum. Her declared plan so far is to poison
the Princess, Creon and Jason, and the Chorus have accepted
their role as accomplices. The first encounter with Jason
shows him up as both cold and passionless, characteristics
which render him wholly unprepared for the revenge on which
she is now working. One thing is missing, a means to avoid
being caught. With the convenient arrival of Aegeus her safe
haven is secured. This is a strange scene, perhaps part comic,
but further evidence of Medea's capacity to fashion and shape
the world round her.

It is only after she has secured Aegeus's sworn oath to
defend her that she finally reveals to the Chorus the shocking
truth that her revenge is to be completed by the murder of
the boys, robbing Jason of his sons. The Chorus are appalled,
'. . . there are laws. We're human. You can't do this'
(ll.812–13). But things are moving fast and their concerns are

brushed aside. The Nurse, who is not part of the conspiracy, leaves to fetch Jason. In this second scene together, a mix of winsome deception and grisly comedy, Medea sets in train the procession to the palace in full knowledge that she has managed to involve, wittingly or unwittingly, virtually the entire cast in the assassination of the King and his daughter.

And so it proves. The gifts of a poisoned robe and tiara are accepted. But in that moment of no return Medea's most human and humane sides almost let her down. Her farewell to her children, fractured by fading resolve and changes of heart, all takes place before she hears the outcome of her plan. When the children return with the Tutor she sends them indoors before the Messenger arrives. She listens exultingly to the appalling description of the death of the Princess in the robe and tiara that stick to her and burn her, then the 'ghastly wrestling-match' with the corpse when Creon tries to rescue his daughter.

The Messenger advises her to escape but when she leaves she goes into the house from where the death cries of the children are soon heard. Jason arrives, already in shock but wholly unprepared for the new disaster the Chorus reveals. As he batters at the locked door, Medea arrives above the action in a dragon chariot supplied by her grandfather, the Sun, the bodies of the two children with her. A prolonged exchange between them shows Medea translated almost to the status of a goddess, Jason defeated and powerless below. Denied even a last request to touch the boys, he is left to live out his remaining years, as Medea foretells, till a spar from the rotting *Argo* will fall and break his skull. Medea meanwhile heads for Athens and her new life.

Commentary

Euripides in his time

Euripides was the third of the three great tragedians of Athens whose work has survived. Aeschylus, born *c.* 525 BC, died in 456. Euripides presented a group of tragedies for the first time at the Great Dionysia the following year. Sophocles, born probably in 496 BC, was more of a contemporary of Euripides, though a few years older, and they died in the same year, 406. There must have been many years when the two were competing for the same dramatic prizes.

The comic playwright, Aristophanes (*c.* 445–*c.* 386 BC), also wrote most of his surviving plays during Euripides' lifetime, using him as a stage character in three and referring to him by name in many of the other surviving ones.

Euripides lived most of his life in Athens but in about 407 moved to Macedon as a guest of King Archelaus. The reason is not recorded but by that time the great war between Athens and Sparta was reaching its final stages and life in the city would have been at best uncomfortable.

455 BC is the date provided from such official records as we have for the first play by Euripides. It was called *The Daughters of Pelias*. None of it has survived, but the title does tell us something. This is the first of a whole series of Euripides' plays to have a woman or women in the title role. Of the eighteen existing tragedies there are thirteen such. More significantly in the present context, the daughters of Pelias figured in the Medea story. It was Pelias, the usurper

of Iolcos, who had sent off Jason to fetch the Golden Fleece. When Jason returned successfully, Medea persuaded Pelias' daughters that they could rejuvenate their father by boiling him in a pot of herbs. Then she gave them the wrong recipe. Medea could well have been a character in that first play. It may be fanciful to conjecture, but it is possible, that in *Medea* Euripides was returning to 'reconsider' a character he had shown at the start of his career in a rather different light.

Nineteen of Euripides' plays have come down to us, including our only complete comic satyr play, *Cyclops*. Ten of his plays survive because they were the most commonly read in the Hellenistic and Roman periods, though *Rhesus* is believed by some critics to have been written by a different but unknown playwright. A further nine are extant as a result of a lucky accident: they were preserved in a manuscript which presents them in a quasi-alphabetical order (they evidently formed one part of a collection representing *The Complete Euripides*). Amongst plays which survive only in fragments, or are known by title from other references, are *Andromeda, Bellerophon, Cadmus, Hypsypyle, Oedipus, Philoctetes, Sthenobaea, Telephus, Theseus* and *Thyestes*.

Euripides won his first dramatic prize in 441 but only three others in his lifetime (including that for the trilogy which contained *Hippolytus*, in 428); the posthumous performances of *Iphigeneia at Aulis*, the lost *Alcmaeon in Corinth* and *Bacchae* in 405 won a further prize. Such relative lack of success in a playwriting career that spanned nearly fifty years was surely the result of the unorthodox views expressed through his plays or by his characters. A fondness for debunking heroic figures, among them generals, politicians and almost anyone in authority, proved more acceptable in subsequent times. He also made women and children, traditional victims, into heroes. In the century after his death he was to become the most performed of all tragedians, living or dead. New productions of his plays were taken on tour throughout the Greek-speaking world. The last hundred years of the present era have seen another surge in his popularity all over the world.

Euripides' approach to playwriting

Euripides is the most realistic of the Greek tragic playwrights but his realism is not confined to situation and language. His characters are vivid, complex and plausible. He has been called, if anachronistically, the first psychologist and such a description is difficult to resist. From him we have the first instance of a guilty conscience (sunesis, in Orestes, l. 396), described as an internal disease rather than an externally imposed punishment. For some this move away from the heroic marks the decline of the tragic form, for others, even in classical times, it appears as a liberation. Longinus, a Roman critic of the first century AD, praised especially Euripides' depiction of madness and love (On the Sublime, 15.3). If in the tragedy of Aeschylus, as is sometimes suggested, the conflicts are at a superhuman level, while in Sophocles it is man or woman confronting divine law, in Euripides human beings have their greatest struggles with themselves. Drama is now internalised, as we see with Medea. Medea is the only person who can defeat Medea. Gods may appear as characters in Euripides but the battleground is that of everyday survival. Inevitably, the position and treatment of women proves a major theme. Greek tragedy shows us many daring and heroic women but none more remarkable than Euripides' Medea, a woman who fights back against her husband and wins, a mother who kills her own children but escapes to begin a new life.

Here and elsewhere Euripides questions traditional beliefs and attitudes, and his plays feature the kind of debates which were common among the intellectuals of the latter part of the fifth century. Strong emotions are expressed and few positions left unchallenged: examples include Hippolytus head to head with his father Theseus in *Hippolytus*; Hecuba challenging Helen in *Trojan Women*; and Peleus debunking Menelaus' reputation in *Andromache*, this last a scene only equalled in its virulence by the slanging match between Andromache and Hermione in the same play. The people of Euripides sound like real people. Such no-holds-barred confrontations worried many critics, especially in the nineteenth and twentieth centuries, and Nietzsche condemned Euripides for just this rationality which he considered a debasement of the noble goals of tragedy.

Such a debate seems to have raged even in fifth-century Athens. Aristophanes' *Frogs*, a play written shortly after the death of Euripides and first performed in 405, centres on a dramatic contest in Hades between a long-dead Aeschylus and the recently-dead Euripides to see which will prove himself the more deserving to return to help save Athens. The stage Euripides complains of Aeschylus as a pedant. The stage Aeschylus condemns the later writer as an innovator and downright immoral: he debunks ancient values and offers the worst possible examples for people to follow. Not too much should be read into such comic creations. Both characters are, of course, inventions of a comic playwright. It is from Aristophanes too that we get the dubious idea that Euripides was a misogynist. Today he seems, rather, to be 'a scientist of the emotions', a dramatist who attempted to understand why the people of myth might have behaved in the way that they did. The picture he offers of Medea, which now seems definitive, concentrates on a woman driven to the act of infanticide, but infanticide is an aspect of the plot which Euripides may have been the first to suggest, as the ultimate revenge against the husband she hates. The complex of emotions that the idea of such an act invokes is handled with extraordinary depth and insight.

Euripides' language is accessible, and at times colloquial, something reflected in the current translation which attempts, nevertheless, to be faithful to the original Greek. His structure varies from the straight narrative (*Orestes, Ion*) to loose and episodic (*Trojan Women, Iphigeneia at Aulis*), but often involves a major turning-point halfway through the action (*Heracles, Andromache*). All take an unexpected angle on the story as known from the existing versions of the myths and from other plays, frequently employing (*Alcestis, Helen*) a comic dimension to question received attitudes. If his characters react in believable ways, he is still tied to the conventions of performance in the Greek theatre, including writing for masked performance and the presence of a chorus. Though some of Euripides' choruses have a pivotal role (*Trojan Women, Bacchae*), most function primarily as interested or engaged witnesses, able to offer advice but, for the most part, indicating a personal relief at being free from the passions which tear the protagonists apart.

Historical context and performance of tragedy

In the early years of the fifth century BC the city-state of Athens was in the process of discovering a novel form of government. In 510 the Athenians had forced out of office the

despotic Hippias, one of the sons of Pisistratus who had set
himself up as tyrant in the year 570. Not that Pisistratus was
a notably harsh ruler. Athens had prospered under his
guidance and the Greek term tyrant, as it was to be used by
Sophocles in the title of his play *Oedipus Tyrannus*, means no
more than 'unconstitutional ruler'. Pisistratus was certainly
that, but when his benevolent reign came to an end in 527
his two sons took joint power. The younger, Hipparchus, was
killed over a love affair and Hippias became so harsh that he
provoked a revolution and had to flee to Persia.

In the years that followed, Athens set about the slow and
painful process of creating a government which would involve
the whole male citizen population. It was to this struggling
world that the three tragic playwrights whose works we have
contributed their plays. In 480 the Persians, defeated ten
years earlier at Marathon in an attempt to reinstate Hippias,
invaded again. Athens was sacked and the people retreated to
the island of Salamis. From there the Athenians tricked the
Persians into an unwise sea-battle which the Athenians won.
Later stories claimed that Aeschylus fought against the Persian
fleet at Salamis; Sophocles sang in the victory celebrations;
and Euripides' mother Clito gave birth on the very day of the
battle.

The thirty-five years that followed saw the processes of
Athenian democracy formalised and systematised. It was a
democracy based on slavery, a democracy based on the
concentration of power exclusively in the hands of male
citizens, a democracy rooted in the extortion of tribute from
communities of the Aegean world in the name of protection
against the almost non-existent threat of the Persians ever
returning. But it did create a political system of free speech,
the power of the vote and eligibility for office to anyone who

possessed the right qualifications. It was certainly closer to anything resembling true democracy than any form of government elsewhere at the time. Euripides' own attitude to the politics and the politicians of his era became more and more hostile, if his plays are anything to go by, as he saw Athens brought to her knees in a war against Sparta where the decisions of the majority proved ever more dubious.

By 458 the latest of the reforms that were to cement this 'democracy' had been put in place. In 462/1 the non-elected Council of the Areopagus had lost most of its powers and divided them among the popular assembly (*Ekklēsia*), the popular law courts (*Dikastēria*) and the council of five hundred (*Boulē*). One of the instigators, Ephialtes, had been assassinated but Pericles had emerged as leader of the democratic faction. Aeschylus' *Oresteia* has a political dimension, the precise interpretation of which is hard to decipher at this range of time, but it may be that he was in favour of the reforms and wrote his most famous trilogy to celebrate the new system. The *Oresteia* was performed in 458. Aeschylus died two years later in Sicily.

The first performance of a tragedy is attributed to Thespis, *c.* 532, in Athens. He had only one actor, who differentiated himself from the chorus. Aristotle was later to suggest in *The Poetics* (*c.* 330 BC) that Aeschylus added a second actor and Sophocles a third, creating more possibilities for interchange and conflict. The three actors were called Protagonist, Deuteragonist, and Tritagonist (first, second, and third actor), and the roles were divided between them. All the actors were male and wore masks, including the chorus. Acting, accordingly, was physical as well as vocal. There were also supernumeraries in non-speaking parts, attendants and children. An actor was called a *hypokrites*, which meant 'one who answers, an interpreter, expounder'.

The theatre space in Athens was eventually able to accommodate up to 17,000 from a population of Attica which is estimated in its entirety at as many as 300,000. The audience would have comprised for the most part male citizens though it is probable that some resident aliens, guests to the city, even some women and children also attended. The two main performance areas were the *orchestra*, usually, though not always, circular; and the *proskenion*, the wide but shallow performance space, probably raised, in front of the *skene*, or 'stage façade'. Most surviving plays require no more than a single setting with a single central doorway, but some do seem to call for a change of setting, or a specific location, and Aristotle also writes that Sophocles introduced 'scene-painting' (*skenographia*) to suggest a representational background.

At the main Athenian dramatic festival, the Great Dionysia, each dramatist put on three tragedies and one satyr play which handled tragic themes comically. A comedy by a different playwright followed. Aeschylus preferred the connected trilogy which allowed the development of a concept such as the workings of divine justice over several generations. Sophocles abandoned the practice of writing connected trilogies and instead preferred to highlight a major character within a single play.

Tragic performances were given annually throughout the fifth century in Athens. The Theatre of Dionysus (the god of theatre) was outdoors and was built into the side of the Acropolis. The chorus, who generally remained present throughout the performance after their first entrance, danced in the *orchestra* as they sang. The audience sat in the *theatron* (literally 'seeing-place'), two-thirds of which bordered on the circumference of the performance area. The music for tragedy was provided by the *aulos*, a reed instrument (like an oboe), and sometimes drums. Spoken portions of the drama, mainly in iambic trimeter, alternated with the choruses, which were in more complex lyric metres and usually arranged in *strophe* and *antistrophe* ('turn' and 'turning back'), possibly referring to their danced accompaniment. The chorus entry was called the *parodos*, as was the walkway between *theatron* and *proskenion* along which chorus or characters could enter. The choral exit was called *exodos*, and the choral sections in between scenes *stasima*.

The spoken part could consist of a monologue called *rhesis*, a dialogue between two or three actors, or some exchange with a chorus. Dialogue in key scenes could be quite realistic, sometimes taking the form of one-line interchange known as *stichomuthia*. At heightened moments an actor might break into a lyric aria, or share in a *kommos*, a formal lament, usually with the chorus.

At first all the actors were non-professional, and the playwright acted too. It is said that Sophocles' weak voice prevented him from acting in his own plays. Gradually acting became more professional and prizes, initially offered only to winning playwrights, were awarded to actors from about the middle of the fifth century. In the fourth and subsequent centuries acting became a highly organised profession, controlled by guilds and providing companies for performances as far away as Sicily, the Middle East and North Africa. For selecting prize-winners in the fifth century, a jury was selected, one from each of the ten tribes in Attica, but to prevent favouritism only a random five of the votes were selected.

Staging was not realistic but the evidence of vase-painting

points to a developed sense of stage grouping and stage picture. Formal tableaux, processions, stage furniture, properties and stage machinery all contributed to a highly visual stage language. Dead bodies, or even interior scenes, could be displayed on a device called the *ekkuklēma*, a kind of stage truck which was rolled out from the central door of the scene-building. The *ekkuklēma* added a dimension of depth. The *mēchanē* ('machine') was a stage crane which allowed aerial entrances and exits, usually of the gods. These two pieces of stage machinery extended the dimensions of the stage, one laterally and one vertically. In later times, but how much later is a matter of dispute, the background could be identified by painted panels (*pinakes*) and by *periaktoi*, prism-shaped scenic units which revolved to display a different picture on each of the three facing surfaces.

The Great Dionysia was held in early spring, traditionally the 9th–13th days of the month *Elaphēbolion* (March/April) when the seas were calm and the visitors from abroad could attend. On the first day of the festival there was an elaborate show of tribute from the allies, war orphans paraded and prominent citizens were given awards. Going to the theatre was a social, civic, and religious event. One purpose of the festival was to impress visiting dignitaries who could include ambassadors from actual or potential enemies.

Three or four days of the Great Dionysia were devoted to plays. Performances began at dawn and lasted all day. Several plays, comedies and tragedies seem to begin in the dark, Aeschylus' *Agamemnon*, for example, and Aristophanes' *Ecclesiazousae*, while the entire action of *Rhesus* is meant to be taking place at night.

Translation

It is never easy for the translator to remain neutral. The good
playwright in most traditions leaves enough flexible for the
director and actor to bring new readings, new emphases
according to the mood and sensibilities of a new occasion. A
translator for the stage needs to do the same but is usually
thought to be under some obligation to remain anonymous,
an interpreter, an intermediary, but someone whose success is
gauged only by the ability to promote the original playwright.
If an ancient play is to live again in our own time and speak
to a contemporary audience, there must be freedom of
interpretation because interpretation is what directing involves.
There is no *Ur*-text, no primary finished version of the
original: there is only the text as blueprint from which the
director fashions the production, while designers and players
make their contribution. Interpretation has to be part of the
process for the director and actor. Interpretation may, indeed
should, also be a part of the process for the translator.

The trouble with dealing with Greek texts is that not only
is the original the province of a diminishing few, but how the
works were actually performed is mainly a matter of
speculation. The Greeks may have subscribed to a stage
language of image, gesture and space but personal academic
preference cannot claim the authority of universal theatrical
truth.

This immediately raises the issue, in translating as well as
in directing plays from ancient Greek, of finding a cultural
context into which they will fit both theatrically and
historically. A hundred years ago the pioneers of the Greek
revival in England were still advocating an antiquarian
approach to Shakespeare's 'Greek' plays, never mind to the
Greeks themselves. In productions a hundred years ago of

Aeschylus, Sophocles or Euripides, every self-respecting hero
would expect to be wearing bronze-age armour. Today's
audiences, informed and enlightened by the imaginative
directors of the contemporary stage, find it easier to make the
leap away from bare knees and sandals. There still seems to
be a reluctance, at least amongst British directors, to free
Greek tragedy from some vague and unfocused sense of 'the
primitive' as the only way of dealing with its 'strangeness',
while at the same time suggesting that there is a single
definitive version of any Greek myth.

The translator's prime task, surely, is to translate what is
there, not invent what isn't. One published translation of
Sophocles' *Antigone* falls into the trap of deciding that a
modern audience will not understand Antigone's concern for
the physical burial of the body of Polyneices and chooses to
add three lines to Antigone's role to explain that, without
burial, Polyneices will be unable to cross the river Styx. To
anyone reading the original it is much more striking that this
is *not* an argument that Antigone ever uses.

All translation is adaptation but it is necessary to make a
distinction at this point between genuine translation and
original work based on existing Greek plays. Innumerable
authors from the Renaissance onwards, aware that the
importance of myth lies in its decoding, have returned to
ancient Greek sources. Several of those who are writing today,
concerned that their target audience would find an original
Greek context obscure and alien have responded by selecting
one or more of the themes of an original Greek tragedy,
usually a Sophocles or a Euripides, and recreating a Greek
play in a cultural context that the new audience will
recognise.

Should the translator do the 'reinterpreting'? Or is it up to the director to decide on the stage iconography? One stage version of one story, the story of Antigone, is powerful because it is specific. The Trojan War may be every war. It may be the Peloponnesian War. It may be the First World War. It may involve NATO bombers or Afghan refugees. On stage the Trojan War is either non-specific, which allows that unspecified war to become whatever war each individual in the audience wants it to be – in other words it is a non-specific macrocosmic metaphor: or, if the director so chooses, it can be this war and now, which becomes a contemporary comment while serving additionally as a microcosm through which to view the whole nature of war. The theatre can work both ways.

In what period and in what country would *Antigone* or *Medea* or *Iphigeneia* not seem relevant? Acts of revenge, acts of treachery, insane cruelty, sacrifice, resistance: any of these, and so many similar, form the spine of the Greek tragic canon. Greek plays should be considered as amenable as any other classic playtexts to uprooting from the original context and relocating in a variety, not only of cultures, but also of periods. After all, the Thebes of Antigone or the Argos of Orestes is as far a cry from fifth-century Athens as are the Ephesus of *The Comedy of Errors* or the Troy of *Troilus and Cressida*. Here the translator does have a role, especially if the production dictates a certain style to which the translator is invited to draw attention.

The twentieth century saw Greek drama rescued from the study where it had so long languished, and restored to the stage. It still took time before the *noli-me-tangere* (keep off!) approach which limited productions gave way to a genuine appreciation that here were dramatic and theatrical texts whose openness offered a special kind of freedom. Greek

drama now forges links that are unique for a theatre which is
open to a wider variety of cultural and performance
approaches than at any time in its history. This is exciting
and productive for designers, directors and actors. But
translation too needs to meet this challenge.

Of course, the plays are old. They come from a period
some of whose terms of reference can be remote, if not
unfathomable. A modern audience has to adjust to the Greek
pantheon, the oracles and the prophets, the sacrifices and the
curses. For the translator there are fundamental decisions to
be made between identifying the nuances of the text and
rendering it playable. It is not just that the theatrical tradition
seems rigid, with its roots in choral dance, masked
performance and civic occasion: minds have opened in the last
thirty years to contemporary cultural values from other
continents which are just as uncompromising.

Verse is one issue: style another. Too much reverence or
too little? Too many English language translations of Greek
plays seem either to lose sight of the original, or lose
sight of the fact that the plays need to be spoken by actors
and for audiences. For translator or director there are,
perhaps, two marks of respect due to a dead playwright. The
first is a legitimate engagement with the text as handed down.
The second is the re-creation, rooted in this original but not
wholly dependent on it, of something for a contemporary
audience which takes account of the past but thrusts it firmly
into the present.

Sometimes a translator will translate a Greek play with a
specific context and a specific production in mind: a
production, in short, where the translator is also the director,
or is working so closely with the director as to be devising a
stage language, in the broadest sense of that term, which will

be equally appropriate to the terms of reference of the
production and to the terms of reference of the original play.

It is precisely where areas of ambiguity exist in performance
that the translator can and does find a voice, and contributes
something much more than a mechanical rendition from one
language into another. Translations have to be understood by
the audiences before whom they are to be performed. They
do not need to sound archaic simply because the plays are
old. These are not 'literary' texts but 'playing' texts, designed
to come alive in the words and actions of the production.

Medea

A husband leaves his wife and two children for another
woman. A familiar scenario, hardly worth writing a play
about, you might think. The story has some refinements. She
is a foreigner: he wants to marry someone from the country
where they now live. She helped him get started: the new wife
will improve his career prospects. She decides to take revenge
through the children: he loses everything.

Common enough, even so, but *Medea* is a play that was
first performed in 431 BC; at a festival in honour of the god
Dionysus; by male actors in masks; in front of an audience of
up to seventeen thousand composed mainly, if not entirely, of
men who believed in their divine right both to treat all non-
Greeks as barbarians and to divorce their wives by a simple
declaration before a witness.

Include alongside the conditions of that first performance
the fact that the husband, Jason, had to harness fire-breathing
bulls and kill a dragon in order to steal a golden fleece, and
that Medea, the first wife, is the granddaughter of the Sun,
and the saga seems to belong exclusively to the world of myth

and legend. Add to the bare bones of the story the nature of
Medea's revenge. She gets her children to deliver a poisoned
robe to the new wife, who happens to be the daughter of the
King of Corinth, killing both the Princess and her father.
Then she murders her own two sons and makes her escape to
Athens in a chariot drawn by dragons. It begins to seem like
a world that we are well out of.

A heady broth, anyway, but a myth that embeds within this
primitive world such perennial appeal that the play has re-
emerged in a series of versions and guises in every era where
the drama has been considered a proper place for the
examination of social and political issues. That is the power of
myth, to create a storyteller's world, a world that never was
but a world that contains such reverberations that anyone and
everyone may decode it in their own particular way. Euripides
was amongst that small number of great playwrights whose
world is bound by neither time nor space.

If the first surviving play of Euripides from 438 offers the
portrait of a wife (*Alcestis*) so devoted as to die on her
husband's behalf, the next we have must have come as a
shock to most of the audience who gathered to see the
production of *Medea* at the Great Dionysia of 431. Alcestis
agreed to sacrifice her own life in her husband's place: Medea
saw to it that her husband's remaining life would be hell. A
mother killing her own children to take vengeance on her
husband is still deeply shocking for an audience.

Plays were presented competitively by three playwrights
chosen at some time the previous year by one of the elected
magistrates known as archons. In 431, a son of Aeschylus
competed with Sophocles and Euripides. Nothing is known of
the level of competition they posed but Euripides certainly
came last with his group of plays that included *Medea*, a

comment, at the very least, on its reception on the day. The play was adventurous in its form as well but it was its subject-matter which must have caused the severest shock.

Whether or not *The Daughters of Pelias* (see page xiii above) included the characters of Jason and Medea, the story of the Argonauts was one that would have been familiar enough. Aeschylus had written an *Argo*, Sophocles wrote a *Pelias* and a *Phrixus*, all likely to have been stories from the same saga. There was at least one epic poem from Corinth written by Eumelus and thought to pre-date the poems of Homer. A fragment of that survives today but we have the whole of the Fourth *Pythian Ode* of Pindar, a contemporary of Aeschylus, in which he traces the history of Cyrene back to one of the Argonauts and, in the process, gives a graphic and heroic account of the quest for the Golden Fleece. The Athenians of 431 would have known their Jason story. What they might not have expected was the Jason created by Euripides.

Jason or Iason – Greek has no letter J – was the legitimate heir to the throne of the Thessalian city of Iolcos. His father Aeson had been dispossessed by a half-brother, Pelias, and Jason was sent away as a child to be brought up in safety on Mount Pelion by Chiron, one of the Centaurs, half man and half horse. The grown-up Jason returned to Iolcos to claim his birthright. Rather than dispose of him outright Pelias agreed to yield the throne if Jason would bring back the Golden Fleece. The quest was assumed to be impossible. The Fleece hung in the grove of Ares in Colchis, a barbaric city at the far end of the Black Sea, and was guarded by a dragon.

Nothing daunted Jason gathered together a group of heroes, amongst whom were said to be Heracles, Orpheus and Theseus. They set out on the ship *Argo* and, after various adventures, arrived at Colchis. The dragon turned out to be

augmented by fire-breathing oxen and a giant snake. And
when Jason had killed the snake a set of armed men grew
instantly from its teeth. At least this is one version of the
story. But Jason had the support of Hera, the wife of Zeus,
and of Athene, and they enlisted Aphrodite. She in her turn
persuaded Eros to fire an arrow of love into the heart of
Medea, the daughter of the King of Colchis. Medea duly fell
in love with Jason and helped him by providing means to
protect himself against the fire-breathing bulls. Eventually he
was able to grab the Fleece and escape with Medea.

Medea may have helped him, as Ariadne helped Theseus
when he went into the labyrinth to fight the Minotaur, but
Jason was still a heroic figure, successful in his quest and
about to return home in triumph. Note, though, how the
Euripidean Medea, albeit at a moment of high passion,
dismisses her husband's heroism:

> I saved your life. There's not a single Greek
> Of those who crewed the *Argo* would deny that,
> When you were sent off to tame fire-breathing bulls,
> To yoke them and sow that deadly field.
> Then there was the dragon, guardian of the Golden Fleece,
> With all its massive coils, never sleeping.
> Who killed it? I killed it and saved your reputation in the
> process. (ll.476–82)

Here is the first key to Euripides' dramatic method. Jason the
hero? Not here. When eventually he offers some response to
Medea he does return to the received myth but in a way that
does him little credit:

> I have to say, as you claim a debt from me,
> That Aphrodite was my protectress on that voyage,
> The goddess, her alone and no one else.
> You're good with words, Medea. Perhaps it seems

Unchivalrous to suggest that it was simply Love
Whose arrows forced you to save my life. (ll.526–31)

The record of Medea's subsequent behaviour is variously told.
In Euripides' play she refers to the murder of her brother,
Apsyrtus, his body cut up and scattered to delay her father's
pursuit. Back in Iolcos she ensured the grisly death of Pelias
at the hands of his own daughters, an act so barbaric that
Jason, far from being heralded as the rightful king, was driven
into exile along with Medea. They eventually found refuge
with King Creon in Corinth where the Euripides play is set.

Medea's ruthlessness and her reputation as a witch were
well established. Her aunt was Circe, the same Circe who in
Homer's *Odyssey* turned Odysseus' men into pigs and left
them like that for a year while she delayed his return home
with her other charms. In *Medea* she refers to magical powers
she has conjured before but uses no more magic than it takes
to mix the deadly ointment she smears on the robe for the
Princess. And when her mind is made up, it is Hecate she
invokes:

Now by Hecate, dark mistress whom I worship,
Partner-in-crime, co-conspirator,
Squatter in the corners of my mind, I swear,
No man damages me with impunity. (ll.395–8)

Hecate was a shadowy goddess, a goddess of the underworld,
a mistress of magic, someone to be wary of. She will turn up
again in drama, two thousand years later, as the leader of the
witches who control Macbeth.

Medea knows what she is doing when she invokes Hecate:

Conjure, Medea, conjure all your craft.
Ooze into evil. (ll.402–3)

Jason, then, is treated less as a hero than as an anti-hero. Medea, on the other hand, may conjure the resources of revenge and turn out capable of murder of her enemies and of her own children but surprisingly little mention is made of her past record, no more than passing references to the death of Pelias or, more notably, to the murder of her brother (Medea off-stage at l.167; a passing reference at l.256; and Jason's accusation l.1334).

There is an important point concealed here, one that an Athenian audience would have taken for granted but of which a modern audience or a modern reader may need to be reminded. What we have in this play – what we have in any Greek play – is what the manuscripts hand down. There are few 'givens', few features of character or situation that we should take for granted because of what we know, or what we think we know, from elsewhere. The popular misconception that the Greeks knew the plots of all the plays they might see is rooted equally in a misunderstanding of how myth functions and in a misunderstanding of how the Greeks viewed their theatre.

A myth is like a skeleton. The bones are in place but what gives individuality, purpose and life itself is what surrounds those bones. The flesh, the organs, the soft and pliable bits are the interesting part, visible and invisible. Once a body has completed its time, what has been a person, whether Euripides himself, Joan of Arc or Martin Luther King, returns to the bones. The bones were always there and they grew with the person. But they changed far less than the outward appearance. It is a shock to a child to realise for the first time that everyone living, breathing, walking and working, carries a skeleton inside. They do. What makes them interesting and individual are the differences, including behaviour, which seldom have anything at all to do with the bone structure. Myth functions like that. And it functioned like that for the Greek playwright.

Certain stories were handed down about people who may or may not have really lived. Whether or not there once was a Medea, a Jason, an Antigone or an Iphigeneia is not of great importance. Nothing that anyone can write about them is going to affect them greatly. As far as the playwright is concerned their stories were simply the bones on which they could build characters and situations. As long as they stuck to the essential outlines so that, for example, Agamemnon does not climb out of his fatal bath and club down Clytemnestra before she can take the axe to him, the playwright could offer all manner of variation. So Heracles, for example, renowned as the strongest of men, could never be a physical weakling. He could be portrayed as a strong man who has lost his strength, as Sophocles shows him in *Women of Trachis*. He could be shown losing his mind, and hence his moral strength, as Euripides depicts him, afflicted by madness in *Heracles*, so that he slaughters his own children.

Helen was known as the most beautiful woman in the world, the cause of the ten-year war against Troy. But Helen in one play could be vain and manipulative, as in *Trojan Women*. Three years later the same playwright, Euripides, could show her in his *Helen* as an unwitting victim who never even went to Troy. The given is her beauty, just as Heracles' given is his strength. So, it was well within the compass of a Greek playwright, and certainly that of Euripides who constantly set out to flout an audience's preconceptions, for a Jason to be shown as less than heroic, Medea driven to infanticide by the way she has been treated.

What all this amounts to is that today's reader needs to be

wary of prejudging any Greek tragedy simply because of what is known about the story from other sources. Characters are not necessarily reliable witnesses, especially when defending themselves against charges levelled at their heads by enemies. But an argument based on what we think Medea may have done or how we believe Jason may have behaved only holds water if the playwright has chosen to include that part of the myth in his particular treatment. Euripides' *Medea* is sufficient unto itself.

Euripides took to beginning his plays, not with an exposition scene, but with a prologue in which one character establishes where and when the play is set, and, on some occasions, how it will end. These prologues are much less of a mechanical device than they might at first seem. They may be delivered by a god, as in *Hippolytus*, *Ion* or *Bacchae*; by a leading character with no more than a partial knowledge of what is going on, as in *Suppliants*, *Andromache* or *Helen*; or by a comparatively humble contributor to events as in *Electra* or *Children of Heracles*. The audience adjusts its perception accordingly. In all cases these speeches are directed, not at any other character in the play, but directly to the audience, a device that tends to lend credibility to what they have to say.

In *Medea* the first tranche of information comes from the Nurse who looks after Medea and Jason's children. After letting the audience know where they are coming in on the story, she offers several pieces of information that affect plot and characters (see page ix under Plot). Of these the two most significant, the ones which prove to supply the central themes of the play, are first Medea's foreignness and secondly her unpredictability:

> She knows now what it means to leave home.
> Anywhere else you're a foreigner,

The children are no consolation. She can't look at them.
God knows what she may do next.
Suffering like that. I know her but she frightens me: (ll.34–8)

This planting of information serves to draw attention to what
will emerge as the two guiding motifs which will permeate the
whole of the play, alienation and revenge. Medea's isolation
indoors is doubly emphasised by the Nurse's next words
'There are the children' (l.47), presumably heralding the
entrance of the two boys or at least their entry into the
audience's circle of attention. Children mean everything to
Jason and to Creon. Survival of the line is paramount. The
notion is underlined by it being the failure to have an heir
that results in Aegeus turning up where and when he does.

If infanticide is the emotive subject of the play, this notion
of Medea's 'difference' serves as a complementary theme in
the playwright's approach to her. The insularity of the
Athenians was one of the factors that united them as a
people. A fierce pride in city was one of the reasons that they
held festivals. The festival of the Great Dionysia was timed to
the spring to remind friends and show foreigners how a
'civilised' community behaved. Beyond this, however, was a
sense that Spartans, Corinthians, Thebans, Thessalians might
not be Athenians but they were Greek, sharing for the most
part a common language and a common set of values. They
might be almost permanently at war with one another but at
least they were Greeks. Outsiders were not Greeks. They were
barbaroi, 'barbarians'. Jason was a Greek, Creon was a Greek.
The Athenian men who watched that first production of
Medea in 431 BC might not have been allowed by the laws of
Athens to marry a Corinthian or a woman from Iolcos. But in
the terms of this play, divorced from, but akin to, the
prevailing social *mores*, a marriage to a Medea was a marriage
to a barbarian, whereas a marriage to a Corinthian would

have offered Jason respectability, never mind status.

Prejudice against the 'barbarian' (anyone who is not Greek) is a significant factor in this play. When Medea does enter she immediately addresses a chorus who are inclined to be sympathetic to her as a deserted wife. 'If you're a foreigner,' she says, 'well, it's best to conform' (l.222). The problem for Medea is overcoming the prejudices of the local women to her as an outsider. This she can only do by trading on their sympathies towards her as a wronged wife:

> There's a wildness, there,
> Something primitive,
> Primitive and wilful. (ll.103–5)

So says the Nurse but the force of the situation dawns fully on Medea only when she confronts Jason and accuses him of keeping her in the dark about his proposed new marriage:

JASON.   Mention the word marriage and look at you.
         You can't control your fury.
MEDEA.   That's not it, is it? As time went on
         You found it inconvenient to have a foreign wife.
         (ll.589–92)

In the original Greek Medea describes herself here as a *barbaron lechos*, a 'barbarian bed/marriage'. Previously in the play she has referred to herself as a *xenos*, an intriguing Greek word that can mean both 'host' and 'guest'. In Corinth that word is as applicable to Jason as to herself. Here, for the first time she recognises herself as a *barbaros*, a non-Greek. In production this can be a moment of supreme revelation, a turning-point where the fury at her desertion turns homicidal. The irony resides in the 'barbarian' respect for oaths and sense of morality, contrasted with Jason's Greek values. From

here on Medea's sense of isolation has developed a new
dimension and she returns to the background she thought she
was escaping, the world of the Sun-god and of Hecate, to
gain her revenge.

All of the other characters in the play try to claim they are
free of prejudice, invariably finding something else to blame.
That is the mountain that Medea has to climb. People expect
her to be strange:

> . . . clever. As an insult,
> Meaning envied, or sullen, or peculiar,
> Or solitary. (ll.303–5)

The subtle dimension Euripides offers is to create a contrast
of temperament between Medea and the Greeks which is
summed up in the attitude of the Chorus, for whom passion
is a thing of danger. The Chorus reflect the Greek 'coolness'
epitomised by the Delphic precept 'Nothing in excess'.
Consider, for example, these two odes:

> Passion. Too much passion.
> No merit in that,
> No reputation there.
> Love, gentle love,
> Is a gift of the gods.
> I'll settle for that.
> With no searing, no poison,
> No obsession, no pain.

> Control. Moderation.
> I'll pray for them,
> I'll be comfortable with them.
> God preserve me
> From that madness,

The affliction that is sex,
Without rhyme, without reason.
Affection, but not passion. (ll.627–42)

The context of that declaration is significant, located immediately after Medea's first confrontation with Jason but heralding the arrival of Aegeus, whom Medea seduces into helping her, with the complicity of the Chorus.

This emotional balancing act between being wary friends and active accomplices in acts of murder is extraordinarily cleverly contrived both by Medea the character and, of course, by Euripides the playwright. The Chorus pronounce themselves profoundly shocked that she should as much as contemplate the murder of her children. When Jason arrives and Medea produces the gifts for the boys to carry to the Princess, who is the Chorus's princess as well as the Princess of Corinth, the Chorus know that Medea is planning not only the murder of the new wife but the murder of her own children too. They do nothing. They reveal nothing. One could respond, of course, by saying that that is what choruses do – nothing. They are not there to initiate action. And there is truth in this. There is still a build-up of sympathy towards Medea in the way she is treated as a woman that makes their refusal to intervene plausible in them, as women.

Medea says her farewell to the children, a farewell in which she changes her mind more than once, after the Tutor returns to tell her that the Princess has accepted the poisoned gifts, but before the Messenger arrives with the news of what happened when she put them on. As she packs the children off indoors this is the Chorus's response, much more than a simple interlude between scenes of high tension:

And I say this. Those who miss out
On experience,
Who never have children,
They're the lucky ones.
They never know, the childless –
They never have the chance –
What a child may bring,
Joy or grief, grief or joy.
The childless never see
That first sweet enchantment
Shrivel, with time, into despair.

How to bring them up.
How to have something to leave them.
Will they turn out frivolous?
Will they turn out decent?
There's no predicting; and no end to it.
But worst, the worst
Of any human experience.
You become prosperous. They grow –
Good children, fine young people –
And then some accident . . .
Death steals them away,
Spirits them underground.
How does anyone survive that?
Why make yourself vulnerable,
Mortals to be toyed with by gods? (ll.1090–1115)

The message here is complex. At one level we have the
'civilised' Greek denial of the world of passion which Medea
represents, a passion which can override even love for your
children and one which the Chorus and the other characters
in the play not only eschew, but cannot begin to comprehend.

Medea's passion frightens them and their reaction is to disavow such emotion. At another level the Chorus, as women and as individuals, are trying to absolve themselves from any involvement in Medea's actions. When it is a matter of Medea's helping Jason because she has fallen in love with him, the myth and Jason himself can blame it on Aphrodite. Perhaps Euripides does so too, as in *Hippolytus* where the two competing goddesses, Aphrodite and Artemis, between them destroy Theseus' wife and son. Medea recognises her own passion all too well, a passion every bit as destructive as the gods and goddesses of other plays.

The only person in the whole of *Medea* who has any real concept of the depth of Medea's feelings is Creon. She tries several ploys to win him round to allowing her one more day in Corinth. Eventually she succeeds and her hard-won success is an interesting contrast to the ease with which she is able to manipulate both her own husband, Jason, and Aegeus, the King of Athens, who offers her a refuge on a blank cheque.

This is another level of Medea's 'difference'. She is imbued with the power to kill a dragon and to persuade the daughters of Pelias to chop up their father and boil him in a pot. She is capable of living in that world of primeval myth and gory revenge. She is also clever enough to manipulate her way round it. Cleverness was a dubious virtue in the Greek world. While heroes might compete to be thought of as *sophos*, 'wise', there was an inbuilt suspicion of someone like Odysseus whose resourcefulness was 'tricky' or 'cunning' rather than displaying the virtues of a proper hero. At the same time it was assumed that the world was divided into friends and enemies. There was no Christian concept of 'loving your enemies', and when Medea admits to hating Jason, or can describe herself to the Chorus as 'a good friend,

but what an enemy' (l.809), these are sentiments which
would appear quite natural to the audience. Using charms
and craft are, as Medea admits, the only weapons she has,
but then a woman's wanting to have a weapon in the first
place makes her suspect in a male society.

It is impossible to try and second-guess the reasons for this
group of plays being placed last in the competition at the
Great Dionysia of 431 BC. Our contemporary reception of a
play may be dictated by the production values. It is also
affected by the attitude of the audience, corporately and as
individuals. If it is nigh on impossible to think one's way into
the mentality of that first-ever audience, this is largely because
that audience was made up of individuals whose own
perceptions would have been affected by all manner of factors
from the number of productions they had witnessed to their
own marital situations. As a deserted wife Medea could expect
some sympathy. The Nurse offers that. So do the Chorus
though they initially seem quite casual about Jason's betrayal.
In their second speech, they, or one of them if this was taken
as a solo line, says:

Your husband's deserted you.
For someone else's bed.
That's not the end of the world. (ll.155–6)

By the end of the play this same Chorus have become
accomplices, whereas the Nurse is not privy to any of
Medea's plans. What causes the difference? Why the change?
Modern actors and a modern director will need to know. The
first production of this translation began with a Chorus of
only three who grew in number as the play progressed to a
final sixteen, the first members gradually converting the
newcomers. Solutions may well be found in Medea's

engagement of their sympathy as women: more, for her treatment as a woman by the men she encounters. Creon simply mistrusts her, but Jason is so callous and patronising as to be the key to allowing Medea to seem today, if not wholly in the right, at least a victim provoked beyond the breaking point.

The list of excuses which Jason dredges up to account for his behaviour make it difficult even to take him seriously:

> . . . my royal marriage,
> That was a clever decision, you must agree,
> As well as a sensible one, the best thing really
> For you and the boys. (ll.547–50)

> You women. You're so fixated. You've convinced yourselves,
> If you're happy in bed, nothing else matters.
> If you're not, then everything's a disaster. (ll.569–73)

> You don't know when you're well off, never have.
> That's your problem. You are so stubborn. (ll.621–2)

> That's my girl. I don't blame you.
> A woman's likely to get a bit emotional
> With her husband marrying again (ll.908–10)

Remarks like these by Jason, including his flouting of his promises to Medea, secure the loyalty of the chorus of women. A male chorus (as in the Theodorakis opera) might have been less sympathetic, though the Tutor in Euripides has little time for the attitudes of his fellow men. Jason's obtuseness, his inability to comprehend anything about the woman to whom he has apparently been married for a good ten years, speaks volumes. His response is laughable, contributing to a whole comic dimension to the text from the series of ironies and misapprehensions. In this, the playwright is as cunning as Medea, seducing the audience, often via the Chorus, into using their privileged knowledge to become partners in the revenge.

It has to be admitted here that part of this may be the result of translation. Any translator will, wittingly or unwittingly, colour the host text with a personal interpretation. Neutrality is not really an option with a language like ancient Greek which does not even share an alphabet with any other country. The most that the Greekless reader can do, and this includes the contemporary Greek for whom classical Greek is only as understandable as might be Chaucerian English to a contemporary English-speaker, is look to more than one translation: or accept that the text of the original may be single but that the various translations do no more than reflect the mass of interpretations available through directorial slant and actors' interpretation. Russians, French and Germans often say how lucky they are to have more than one Shakespeare whereas the English-speaking world has to make do with the single original. Maybe any modern view of Sophocles or Euripides is similarly fluid for those who approach the work through translation. And maybe this is no bad thing for the art of the theatre, rooted, as it is, in a performance ethic where no two productions will ever be the same. It provides too a link through to the way in which the Greek playwrights returned again and again to the same myths in order to reappraise them.

Euripides has sometimes been accused of writing himself into a corner in his plays and having to resort to a mechanical device, the *deus ex machina*, 'a god from the machine', in order to provide a proper ending. No such accusation is made against *Medea*, though Medea escapes in her flying chariot, a *dea in machina*. The ending is certainly uncompromising,

uncomfortable too. Gilbert Murray, the first great populariser
of Euripides in English, acknowledged in 1914 in the
introduction to his translation what he called the
'concentrated dramatic quality and sheer intensity of passion'
in the play but suggested that 'there are not many scholars
who would put it among their favourite tragedies'. More
recent opinion might seem to disagree if the exceptional
number of professional and student productions of the last
twenty years is any guide.

The ending can still seem morally perplexing. Any
experienced reader of plays or member of a modern audience
can trace Euripides' dramatic structure without difficulty. The
process of exposition; the introduction and dramatic
'exploitation' of the children; use of minor characters; the
Chorus; Medea's confrontations with Creon and Aegeus; the
two scenes with Jason: all of these have a recognisable
dramatic shape and impact which make the play seem more
modern in concept and execution than any other Greek
tragedy. The build-up to the murder of the Princess and the
death of her father, Creon, have that quality of the inexorable
that can hold any audience. The description by the Messenger
of their terrible end and Medea's resolution to murder the
two boys continue the fearsome process till the cries are heard
off-stage as the children try to escape.

Jason arrives, shocked only by what has happened in the
palace. The Chorus tell him that Medea has killed their
children indoors but before he can break into his house,
Medea appears above the action with the bodies of the
children in a chariot drawn by a dragon. A scene of almost a
hundred lines between Jason and Medea is marked by a
display of grief from Jason matched by apparent detachment
from Medea. This curious mixture of domestic squabble and

prophetic utterance is difficult for a modern audience,
especially as it reaches no denouement beyond a few lines
from the Chorus about the moral of the story, lines which are
used identically by Euripides to end four others of his plays.

There are three sources of concern about this ending. The
first is purely mechanical. Why end a play, which may be
about kings and queens, but is at root a domestic tragedy, by
having one of the characters arrive in mid-air in such
spectacular circumstances? Even Aristotle had reservations
about this one. Secondly, why, if she is now effectively a god
who can forecast Jason's eventual death, does Medea argue
with her husband so naively about whether or not she was
justified in killing the children to punish him? And thirdly,
how and why is she allowed to get away with this murder?

A single answer can serve to address, if not assuage, all
three concerns. The Greek theatre of the time employed two
stage devices to enhance the stage action and extend the
dimensions of the stage. The first of these was the *ekkuklēma*,
a stage 'truck' on which the results of off-stage actions could
be revealed to the audience. When the death cries of
Agamemnon are heard off-stage, for example, in Aeschylus'
Agamemnon this is a prelude to his body being introduced in
tableau. Medea has entered her house. Jason beats at the
doors, trying to gain entry. The audience seems to be led to
expect the opening of the doors to reveal the dead children.
Instead the children and their mother are translated from
earthly level to the divine by the use of the other stage device,
the crane or *mēchanē*. This was employed to fly in immortal
characters, usually gods or goddesses who signified their status
by their stage position above the action.

Euripides makes use of this device in many of his
subsequent plays, including the posthumous *Bacchae* where

Dionysus who has spent most of the play 'disguised as a man' arrives in epiphany. The Medea of most of the play is primarily an abused wife who undertakes a drastic revenge on an unfaithful husband. But this is more than a tale of an unsuccessful marriage. The Medea of myth does have divine connections. Her world was one of dragons and dragon-chariots. She does possess powers beyond those of ordinary mortals and this is part of why and how the Greek characters are incapable of comprehending her nature.

Medea gets away with it. She kills a king's daughter, and the king, and her own children. If this were a Shakespeare play there would be no way she would escape. In Shakespeare killers get their comeuppance. This is not Greek morality and the play is all the more uncomfortable for it. It is the mark of her power and the power of her feelings that she can be transformed into her own *dea ex machina*. In this last scene, sympathy is perhaps engaged for Jason for the first time – he has certainly cut a poor figure when justifying himself to his wife. But she is now more than his wife. She is empowered both by the refuge she has organised for herself in Athens and by the declaration of her semi-divine status with the provision of a divine means of escape.

The transformation is abrupt but not so abrupt that there is not still part of her which wants to justify what she has done by blaming the man for the position into which he forced her. If she is above displaying grief for the children at this point this is not to disavow the torments through which she travelled in making the decision to kill them and executing that decision. This ending allows the myth to continue with Medea's escape to Athens. It piles the responsibility on to Jason as the survivor of a series of miscalculations as shocking as those which bring down the Creon of Sophocles' *Antigone*.

Death is not always the worst fate that the Greek playwrights can devise. 'Wait until you are old,' says Medea. Living with the consequences of your actions creates the world of nightmare.

Brief textual history

There were regular revivals of Euripides' work after his death. Hundreds of years later the Romans still prized Euripides. Ennius (239–169 BC) wrote adaptations including *Medea*; as did Accius (170–?86 BC). Half of the plays by Seneca (?1–65 AD) have parallels in Euripides, one of them a *Medea*.

Greek tragedy became known in the West mainly through Latin translations, and came to Shakespeare via Seneca. *Medea* was first actually printed in Greek in Florence about 1494.

Brief performance history

A comprehensive study Medea in Performance *is recommended in the bibliography. It contains a complete record of all known productions between 1540 and 2000.*

The Medea of Euripides was almost certainly not the first stage Medea but did become the definitive version. From the fourth century BC onwards the play was being revived not only at festivals in Greece but by the touring companies that sprang up and worked a provincial circuit which stretched in time from Medea's own home to all corners of the Roman Empire.

Seneca's *Medea* was probably never intended for a stage production, certainly not in any of the spectacular theatres which the Romans built for a variety of only marginally dramatic events. The speeches are of great length. Two of them take up the entire third act. The subtleties of dramatic dialogue go by the board but in compensation there is a concentrated power and intensity appropriate to the story.

The seventeenth and eighteenth centuries saw a wide variety of versions, including musical ones. By the nineteenth century Medea found her way on to the burlesque stage, two comic versions opening on the same day in London in 1856.

Medea's has proved to be a popular story in opera, appealing especially to the eighteenth and twentieth centuries. Here, possibly, a taste for violence accompanied modernity. Marc-Antoine Charpentier in his *Médée* (1693), set to a text by Thomas Corneille, and Luigi Cherubini in 1797 both retained the tragic ending. Mikis Theodorakis' *Medea* (1991) is a parable for the history of Greece.

There were a whole host of twentieth-century performances, translations and adaptations of Euripides' plays. Max Reinhardt directed a German translation in 1904 and Gilbert Murray's translation with Sybil Thorndike toured to South Africa in 1929.

In the Russian director Nikolai Oklopkhov's production of *Medea* (1962), Medea was treated as a social victim, but some critics chose to see a parallel between her and Stalin, both Georgians, both 'murderers of their children'. Jean Anouilh's *Médée* is an original play, first performed in 1953, a long one-act piece whose guiding motif is a marriage embarked upon solely from physical love, the passing of which has left a residue of passion that has become wholly destructive. The *Medea* of Franca Rame and Dario Fo is no more than five pages long but takes the parable into a new dimension on the emancipation of women. There have been performances of Euripides' play in modern times in Greece

since 1868, prominent among them starring vehicles for
Katina Paxinou in 1958 and Aspasia Papathanasiou in several
productions since 1962 up to her own production in 1989.

The play has often been seen to exemplify social protest.
Hans Henry Jahnn first cast a black actor, Agnes Straub, in
the role in Germany in 1926. In the 1960s Guy Butler wrote
a *Demea* (an anagram of *Medea*), which could not be
performed in South Africa because of the restrictions until
1990 on multiracial casting.

Heiner Müller's *Medeamaterial* (1983) set his parable in the
aftermath of the Second World War (this was produced by
Theodoros Terzopoulos in 1988). Yukio Ninagawa's Japanese
production of *Medea* in 1978 was more faithful to Euripides'
original text, but combined it with the techniques of Noh and
Kabuki drama. Brendan Kennelly's *Medea* (1991) shows Jason
as a stand-in for Britain and Medea for Ireland.

There have been a number of films based on *Medea*, among
them Pasolini's *Medea* (1967) which treated the myth behind
the play in psychological and anthropological terms. Jules
Dassin's *Dream of Passion* (1978) is about an actress (Melina
Mercouri) rehearsing the role at the same time as becoming
fascinated by a contemporary parallel. Lars von Trier's film,
made for television in 1988, tells the whole story almost
entirely in film images and with a minimum of dialogue.

Further Reading

Editions of the plays

The standard text in Greek, on which this translation is based, is:

Diggle, James (ed.), *Euripidis Fabulae*, Vol.1, Oxford, Clarendon Press, 1984

There are many translations of the extant tragedies and comedies including:

Walton, J. Michael (ed.), *Classical Greek Dramatists* (all 46 Greek tragedies and comedies in 13 volumes), London, Methuen, 1988–2000

Grene, David, and Lattimore, Richmond, *The Complete Greek Tragedies*, Chicago, University of Chicago Press, 1953–

Also, volumes of selected tragedies and comedies in the Penguin Classics and Dent Everyman series

General bibliography

Arnott, P.D., *Public and Performance in Ancient Greece*, London, Routledge, 1989

Barlow, Shirley, *The Imagery of Euripides*, London, Methuen, 1971

Bates, W.N., *Euripides: A Student of Human Nature*, Oxford, OUP, 1930

Clauss, James J., and Johnston, Sarah Iles (eds), *Medea: Essays on Medea in Myth, Literature, Philosophy and Art*, Princeton, Princeton University Press, 1997

Conacher, D.J., *Euripidean Drama, Myth, Theme and Structure*, Oxford, OUP, 1967

Green, J.R., *Theatre in Ancient Greek Society*, London, Routledge, 1994

Hall, Edith, Macintosh, Fiona, and Taplin, Oliver (eds), *Medea in Performance: 1500–2000*, Oxford, Legenda, 2000

Halleran, M.R., *Stagecraft in Euripides*, London, Croom Helm, 1985

Hourmouziades, N.C., *Production and Imagination in Euripides*, Athens, Greek Society for Humanistic Studies, 1965

Lefkowitz, Mary R., *Women in Greek Myth*, Baltimore, Johns Hopkins University Press, 1986

Lucas, F.L., *Euripides and his Influence*, London, Harrap, 1924

McDonald, Marianne, *Euripides in Cinema: The Heart Made Visible*, Philadelphia, Centrum, 1983

—— *Ancient Sun, Modern Light: Greek Drama on the Modern Stage*, New York, Columbia University Press, 1992

—— *Sing Sorrow: Classics, History and Heroines in Opera*, Westport, Greenwood, 2001

Murray, Gilbert, *Euripides and his Age*, 2nd edition, Oxford, OUP, 1947

Pomeroy, Sarah B., *Goddesses, Whores, Wives and Slaves: Women in Classical Antiquity*, London, Pimlico, 1994

Stanford, W.B., *Tragedy and the Emotions*, London, Routledge, 1983

Vellacott, Philip, *Ironic Drama: a Study of Euripides' Method and Meaning*, Cambridge, CUP, 1975

Walton, J. Michael, *Greek Theatre Practice*, Westport, Greenwood, 1980; 2nd ed., London, Methuen, 1991

—— *The Greek Sense of Theatre: Tragedy Reviewed*, London, Methuen, 1984; 2nd ed., Amsterdam, Harwood Academic Publishers, 1996

Wiles, David, *Greek Theatre Performance: An Introduction*, Cambridge, CUP, 2000

Wolf, Christa, *Medea: A Modern Retelling*, intro. by Margaret Atwood, trans. John Cullen, New York, Doubleday, 1998

Zimmermann, B., *Greek Tragedy: An Introduction*, trans. T. Marier, Baltimore, Johns Hopkins University, 1991

MEDEA

translated by J. Michael Walton

Characters

NURSE *of Medea's children*
TWO SONS *of Medea and Jason*
TUTOR
MEDEA
CHORUS OF LOCAL WOMEN
CREON, *King of Corinth*
JASON
AEGEUS, *King of Athens*
MESSENGER

Note. Off-stage speeches (Medea and children) were transmitted phonetically from the Greek in the first production of this translation. A transliteration is included in this version.

The line numbering alongside the text relates to the Greek original rather than the English translation.

Corinth. Outside the house of Jason. Enter the NURSE.

NURSE. If only. If only the good ship *Argo*[1]
    Had never negotiated the misty cliffs,
    Never beached at Colchis. If only.
    If only no forester had ever chopped the wood,
    No carpenter fashioned oars,
    For all those fine young men
    Whom Pelias sent to find the Golden Fleece.
    Then Medea, my mistress, would never have sailed for Iolcos,
    Besotted with her Jason.
    Never have persuaded those daughters of Pelias[2]   10
    To kill their father. Nor had to flee here,
    To Corinth with her man and with their children.
    Oh, people liked her. Exile was bearable.
    And Jason. She did everything for Jason.
    The strongest fortress you can find,
    A woman and a man in partnership.
    Till now.

    Now love's betrayed, corrupted, turned to hate.
    Jason, the traitor, is leaving them, wife and family,
    To bed down with a princess, Creusa, Creon's child.
    A proper marriage.
    So Medea, poor Medea, is cast aside   20
    She curses him, calling on the vows they made,
    Imploring the gods to see his perfidy.
    She won't eat. Just lies there suffering.
    She can't stop crying.
    From the moment she heard how he'd betrayed her,
    She hasn't as much as raised her head.
    Her friends might as well talk to a stone or to the sea
    As expect her to listen to them.
    Just, now and then, a twist of the head   30
    Recalling the father she loved, her country,
    The home she gave up.

All for this man who's now had enough of her.
She knows now what it means to leave home.
Anywhere else you're a foreigner,
The chidren are no consolation. She can't look at them.
God knows what she may do next.
Suffering like that. I know her but she frightens me:

40   In case she sharpens a knife for her own heart,
Creeping silently through the house to her bed,
Or tries to kill the king, or the new bridegroom,
Provoking some irreparable disaster.
She's an odd one.
You'd be a fool to cross her lightly.
Enter the CHILDREN.
There are the children. They've been playing ball.
A mother's problems hardly trouble children.
Young hearts can't concentrate on grief.
Enter the TUTOR.

TUTOR. You silly old woman. You're just a piece of property.
50   What do you think you're doing out here,
Telling the world your troubles?
Medea needs you, doesn't she? In there.

NURSE. And you're a silly old man.
You may be the children's guardian
But aren't decent servants meant to feel anything
When disaster strikes the household?
All this. It's so upsetting.
I had to talk to someone about poor Medea,
Even if it's just the earth and the sky.

60 TUTOR. Has she stopped then? Stopped crying?

NURSE. You'd be lucky. Hardly started yet.

TUTOR. Daft. I shouldn't call her that, I know,
But she doesn't know the half of it.

NURSE. What are you on about, you old fool? Out with it.

TUTOR. Nothing. Nothing. I shouldn't have spoken.

NURSE. I'm not having this. We're both slaves, you know.
I'm not going to tell anybody, if I don't have to.

TUTOR. Well, I was pretending not to listen,
But I did hear someone say – down by the fountain

Where the old gaffers play dominoes[3] –
That Creon means to send them packing, 70
Mother and children, away from Corinth.
That's what someone said but who can tell?
You know how these stories get about.
I just hope this one's wrong.

NURSE. What about Jason? He may have his differences with
                                        Medea
But he's not going to let the boys suffer, is he?

TUTOR. You know what they say. New shoes run quicker than old.
But there's not many will stick up for him round here.

NURSE. That's us done for too, you realise.
A new problem to take on board, before we've unloaded the
                                        last.

TUTOR. Hey. Listen, now. Not a peep out of you. 80
Not a word to the mistress. Understood?

NURSE. Poor boys. Did you hear that? That father of yours . . .
What a bastard. He may be my master
But not even a friend could defend him. He's rotten.

TUTOR. Who isn't? Where've you been all your life?
Everyone's interested in number one.
You'll find the odd just man, but few and far between.
Children can't compete with a new girlfriend.

NURSE. There now, boys. Don't you fret. In you go.
Just keep them out of the way, will you? 90
Don't let them go near their mother in this mood.
I didn't like the way she glared at them.
She looked dangerous. And I know her.
This mood's explosive. Someone's going to suffer.
Let's hope it's an enemy not a friend.

MEDEA (*off*). No! No! No![4]
Let me die.
[*iô*
dustanos egô melea te ponôn
iô, moi moi, pôs an oloiman?]

NURSE. Hear that, children?
Your mother's in trouble.
She's upset. Angry. Off you go.

100   Indoors. Quickly.
            And don't let her set eyes on you.
            In you go. Careful now.
            There's a wildness there,
            Something primitive,
            Primitive and wilful.
            Quickly. Indoors.
            In a proud spirit
            A distant cloud of grief
            Can grow into a torrent.
            What next?
            Mercurial.
            Unpredictable.
110   How will such a spirit react?
      MEDEA (off). Pain.
            Hate.
            Cursed womb.
            Accursed children
            From such a father.
            [aiai,
            epathon tlamôn epathon megalôn
            axi' odurmôn. ô kataratoi
            paides oloisthe stugeras matros
            sun patri, kai pas domos erroi.]
            Enter the CHORUS.
      NURSE. Poor things. No!
            Why blame the children for the father's sin?
            Why hate them?
            Children, I fear for you.
            The temper of the tyrant
            Can be a fearful thing.
120   A habit of power
            Condones viciousness.
            Better the quiet life.
            I'll settle for mediocrity
            With peace of mind,
            Moderation the watchword.
            Ambition brings its own return,

   God's envy. Further to fall.   130
CHORUS. I heard her voice.
   I heard her crying, poor foreign queen.
   MEDEA, off, sound of weeping.
CHORUS. There. Again.
   Old woman, tell me,
   I heard through the door
   That awful sound of sorrow.
   Such misery strikes to the heart.
   This has been a good house.
NURSE. House. A house but no longer a home.
   All gone.
   The man aspires to a bed in the palace.   140
   So she lives out her life in her room,
   Inconsolable.
MEDEA (*off*). A lightning bolt through the brain.
   I'd welcome that.
   What possible reason for living?
   Please death, please free me from this life,
   Become intolerable.
   [*aiai
   dia mou kephalas phlox ourania
   baiē; ti de moi zēn eti kerdos?
   Pheu, pheu! thanatô katalusaiman
   biotan stugeran prolipousa.*]
CHORUS. Lord of the earth and lord of light,
   Did you hear that?
   She sounds distraught.   150
   Why seek to welcome death,
   Poor woman? It hurries quick enough.
   Don't spur it on.
   Your husband's deserted you.
   For someone else's bed.
   That's not the end of the world.
   God will work it out.
   You mustn't take so hard the loss of a husband.
MEDEA (*off*). Goddess of justice, goddess of childbirth,[5]   160
   Look down on me and my pain.

We made promises.
Now he's broken his.
I want her dead.
I want the pair of them obliterated,
Burnt to death in their own home,
Who dared to do me damage.
Oh my father! Oh my home that I abandoned!
Forgive me for the brother that I killed.[6]
[*Ô megala Themi kai potni' Artemi,
leusseth' ha paschô, megalois horkois
endēsamena ton kataraton
posin? Hon pot' egô numphan t'esidoim'
autois melathrois diaknaiomenous,
hoi' eme prosthen tolmôs adikein.
ô pater, ô polis, hôn apenasthēn
aischrôs ton emon kteinasa kasin.*]

NURSE. Do you hear that?
    She calls on Zeus and Themis,
170   The gods who secure promises.
    She'll not take this lying down.

CHORUS. Perhaps she might come out.
    And then, perhaps, she'd listen
    To what we have to say,
    We could suggest that she control
    That temper of hers.
    I can always advise a friend, I hope.
180   Go on into the house
    And bring her out.
    Tell her we're all friends here.
    Hurry, before she does something stupid.
    This sort of grieving gets out of control.

NURSE. I doubt if I can persuade her,
    But I'll try, if it will make you happy.
    She's like a wild animal with the servants,
    A lioness, protecting her cubs,
    When anyone as much as speaks to her.
190   Those old bards missed the point,
    Celebrating the joyful things in life

In comfort at feasts and festivals.
Instead they should have tried
To soothe away life's misery and pain,
For families racked by misfortune or by death.
Music should offer consolation.   200
What does it do? Protects the well-fed
By papering over the cracks.
Exit NURSE.

CHORUS. I heard her.
    I heard that ecstasy of grieving
    Directed at the traitor to her bed.
    She calls on the gods to avenge her wrongs,
    Protectors of the promise
    Which brought her over the salt and murky sea   210
    Here to Greece where that oath was broken.
    Enter MEDEA.

MEDEA. There now. I've come outside.
    I wouldn't want to be reproached, my Corinthian friends,
    For being high and mighty. Indoors and aloof.
    If you like a quiet life they'll call you antisocial.
    But when were first impressions reliable?
    One man will hate another for no reason
    The moment he sets eyes on him.   220
    A gut reaction but where's the justice in that?
    If you're a foreigner, well, it's best to conform.[7]
    Even a citizen can't make the rules
    Simply to suit himself. That would be bad manners.
    But I . . . I was not expecting this.
    It pierces me to the soul.
    You are my friends. I've lost the will to live.
    My life was centred on one man, my husband.
    A hollow man.
    Poor women.   230
    No living, breathing creature feels as we do.
    We want a husband? It's an auction
    Where we pay to give away our bodies.
    That's not the half of it. A good man or a bad?
    By the time you find that out it's too late.

Divorce for a woman means disgrace.
And once she's married, there's no saying 'no'.
It's her who has to change the patterns of her life.
You'd need to be clairvoyant
240   To know how to behave in bed.
If you do strike lucky
And this husband turns out bearable,
Submits gracefully, then fine. Congratulations.
If not, you might as well be dead.
When a man starts to get bored at home
He can visit a friend, some kindred spirit,
Look for consolation elsewhere.
We have a single focus, him.
You've a nice, easy life, that's what they say,
Safe at home when they're off fighting.
Good thinking, that is, isn't it?
250   I'd fight three wars rather than give birth once.
Our situations are different, of course.
This is your city. Your father's house was here.
Life at its best, with your friends around you.
But I'm alone, stateless, abused
By a husband like something picked up abroad.
No mother. No brother. No relation
To turn to in a time of trouble.
That's why I'd like to ask for your support.
260   If I hit upon some means, some stratagem,
To pay my husband back for what he's done,
The bride and giver of the bride he means to marry,
Say nothing.
A woman's always full of fears, of course,
Petrified by the mere sight of steel.
But scorn her, cross her in love,
And savour the colour of her vengeance.
CHORUS. Of course. Pay him back, Medea.
That's only fair. You suffer. Why shouldn't you?
Look out – Creon. Here comes the king.
270   Some new development.
Enter CREON.

CREON. I know that sullen look directed at your husband.
   I want you out of here, Medea,
   Out of this country and those boys with you.
   And I want it now. I've made a decision.
   I'm not returning home until you've gone.
MEDEA. I'm helpless. What do you expect me to do?
   Everyone against me. No refuge.
   Creon, I have done nothing.   280
   Why are you banishing me?
CREON. Because you frighten me.
   I'll not mince words. I'm frightened
   You might devise some mischief against my daughter.[8]
   And do you know why I'm frightened?
   Because you're clever. And you're capable of anything.[9]
   You've been kicked out of your husband's bed
   And you're angry. I've heard your threats –
   They told me – against the bride, the groom,
   All of us. So I'm taking no chances.   290
   Rather your hatred now than regret later.
MEDEA. Clever? I've been called that before, Creon.
   I've a reputation, haven't I, for causing trouble?
   No man in his right mind
   Should teach his children to be clever.
   No point in being cleverer than the next man.
   People don't like it. They get jealous.
   Try new ideas on idiots and they'll hate you.
   So, what's the point?
   Become more famous than the sages,   300
   They'll hate you more than ever.
   I do speak from experience here.
   Yes, I'm called clever. As an insult,
   Meaning envied, or sullen, or peculiar,
   Or solitary. Well, I'm not that clever.
   So you're afraid of me, Creon.
   What am I going to do that's so terrible?
   I can't do much to damage a king.
   And why harm you? Did you harm me?
   You gave your daughter to the man of your choice.   310

      True I hate my husband, but you did something sensible.
      I don't grudge you your prosperity.
      As for their marriage – good luck to it.
      Just let me stay. I'm the victim here,
      But you can't argue with power. I'll keep quiet.
  CREON. It all sounds very docile,
      But what's going on inside that head of yours?
      Something nasty. I trust you less than ever.
      You know where you are with a hothead, woman or man.

320   They're easier to fathom than the silent types.
      Go. Now. Without another word.
      It's decided. You're a baleful influence here.
      No trick you pull can change that.
  MEDEA. Please. I beseech you. In your daughter's name.
  CREON. Don't waste your breath.
  MEDEA. I'm begging you.
  CREON. My family come first.
  MEDEA. My country! My country!
  CREON. *My* country! *My* country and *my* family.

330 MEDEA. Oh, the curse that is love.
  CREON. Depending on the circumstance.
  MEDEA. The cause. For god's sake remember the cause of this.
  CREON. Take yourself off. You're nothing but trouble.
  MEDEA. Trouble, yes. Trouble and more trouble.
  CREON. Do you want the servants to throw you out?
  MEDEA. Please, Creon!
  CREON. You're making a scene.
  MEDEA. I'll go. I'll go. Just one thing. Please.
  CREON. Then go. Why make such a fuss about it?

340 MEDEA. One day. Let me stay one more day.
      I need time to think about banishment.
      The children. To make provision for the children,
      Since their father can't be bothered,
      Take pity on them. You're a father yourself.
      You must show some humanity.
      I'm not worried about myself.
      Exile is exile but for them it's a disaster.
  CREON. I'm not a bully. It's not in my nature.

And I paid for it in the past.
This time too, probably.   350
Yes. All right. But I give you fair warning –
If the light of tomorrow's dawn finds your sons
Or you within our borders, it's death.
That's final. Stay a last day if you must.
You can't get up to much mischief in one day.
Exit CREON.

CHORUS. Poor woman.
    Trouble on top of trouble.
    Where are you to turn?
    Where do you look for protection?
    For a welcome or a home?   360
    That's where some god has left you,
    Medea, rudderless in a storm.

MEDEA. Everything against me. So be it.
    We're not finished yet. Oh no.
    A gruesome coupling awaits this bridal pair.
    A sour wedding breakfast for the guests.
    I'd not suck up to him, unless I needed to,
    For what I'm planning. Not a word, not a touch.
    You'll see that, I'm sure.   370
    The fool!
    When all my plans are hanging by a thread
    He offers me a day before my banishment,
    A day for me to transform the father and the daughter
    And my husband, three enemies into three corpses.
    A thousand deaths I have for them, dear friends.
    Where would be a good place to start?
    Fire the palace during the reception?
    Steal into the bridal suite
    And knife them *in flagrante*?   380
    One thing stops me. I might get caught.
    If they found me in the palace, red-handed,
    It's me who'd die, a mockery, a laughing-stock.
    Surest is safest. Stick to what you do best.
    Where's my expertise? In poison.
    A death sentence for them. But what about me?

What city will take me in, grant me asylum,
A home, security from avengers?
Nothing. Nowhere. Slowly now. Bide your time.
390   You want to get away with this.
Cunning. That's what these murders need.
And stealth. If I should fail . . . I'll take the sword
And turn it on myself. Suicide takes courage.
Now by Hecate, dark mistress whom I worship,[10]
Partner-in-crime, co-conspirator,
Squatter in the corners of my mind, I swear,
No man damages me with impunity.
They'll rue this wedding-day I send them,
400   Rue their vows and rue my exile.
To the task, then.
Conjure, Medea, conjure all your craft.
Ooze into evil. Hold hard like a limpet.
Concentrate on grievance.
What jokes they'll make at the wedding,
Those Corinthian men. You can't have that,
You, a princess, a granddaughter of the Sun.[11]
You have the knowledge, Medea.
After all, we women are good for nothing –
That's what they say – except causing trouble.
410   CHORUS.   Rivers flow backwards,
What's right is wrong,
Corrupt counsel prevails:
There's no faith in god,
Because of men.
But times are changing:
Our deeds will be glorified.
An end to those slanders,
420   Celebration of women.

And all those old songs
With their stories of faithlessness,
Enough of them.
Apollo, god of music,
Gave his talent to men,
Excluding us women.

Had he not, I'd write songs,
New songs about heroines,
Not heroes but women.   430

But you left your home,
Passion in your heart,
Past the twin rocks
To a foreign country.
Suddenly waking
With your marriage in tatters,
Poor Medea, an exile,
Humiliated.

The sanction of a promise. Gone.
Shame at bad faith. Gone.
Nowhere in Greece,   440
Dispersed to the skies.
And for you, poor Medea,
No home to run to,
Your bed usurped,
Dispossessed.

Enter JASON.

JASON. If I've seen it once I've seen it a hundred times.
   Bad temper means trouble.
   You could have stayed here, you know,
   If you'd just knuckled down to do what you're told.
   Instead you've talked yourself into exile.   450
   So unnecessary. Well, it's no skin off my nose.
   You can tell the world what a swine Jason is.
   But all that against the royal family,
   You're lucky they only banished you.
   I've done everything I could, believe me.
   I never wanted you to have to leave.
   But denouncing them as tyrants,
   You must be off your head. Exile? Serve you right.
   Anyway, I don't bear grudges against loved ones.
   We need to think about your future. That's why I've come.   460
   We can't have you destitute, not with the children,
   It can be difficult, exile. All manner of problems.

So, hate me if you like, but I bear no grudge against you.
MEDEA. You bastard! Coward! Would there were words
. To describe your cowardice.
    You come here? You dare come here to me?
    Perjured, lying bastard.
    A real hero, aren't you, bold enough
470 To destroy your family and then face them out.
    A legion of diseases prey on men,
    But gall like yours is worse than a disease.
    I'm glad you came, though. It gives me the pleasure
    Of telling you what I think of you. Enjoy it.
    Where to begin, that's the problem.
    I saved your life.[12] There's not a single Greek
    Of those who crewed the *Argo* would deny that,
    When you were sent off to tame fire-breathing bulls,
    To yoke them and sow that deadly field.
480 Then there was the dragon, guardian of the Golden Fleece,
    With all its massive coils, never sleeping.
    Who killed it? I killed it and saved your reputation in the

                                                        process.

    It was me betrayed my father and my home
    To land at Iolcos by Mount Pelion,
    Fond as I was, fonder than was wise.
    I caused the death of Pelias, a terrible death
    At his children's hands, but all for you.
    That's what I did for you and what's your rotten response?
    Betrayal when you fancy some new wife.
490 I bore your children. Had I not,
    You might have had excuse at least.
    You broke your oath. Do you believe in gods,
    You know those old-fashioned gods who used to be in control?
    Or do you think men make the rules these days?
    You broke your word to me.
    By this right hand you used to hold,
    Upon my knees I say 'You used me'
    And I feel dirty from your touch.

    Let's talk like friends, shall we,
500 Though I hardly expect fair treatment here.

Still. Your response should be revealing.
Where do you expect me to go? Back to my father's house?
The one I betrayed when I left with you?
To the daughters of Pelias, poor things, perhaps?
They'd have a welcome, I'm sure, for their father's killer.
That's it, you see. My friends are all enemies.
Because of all those dreadful things I did.
Because of all the dreadful things I did for you.
I do have a wonderful social position
Among Greek women. And a distinguished husband   510
Of course, an honourable man. But if I'm exiled,
Dear me, what then? And wander off with the children
All alone? People will talk. 'A new bridegroom, he may be,
But the children are begging, and the woman who made him.
You showed us, Zeus, how to tell gold from counterfeit.
Pity you didn't brand men to show the same.'

CHORUS. There's an anger that goes beyond all remedy   520
When love turns to hate.

JASON. I'd best restrain myself, I think,
And like a good helmsman on a ship
Reef in the sail and run before the storm
Of that unfettered tongue of yours.
I have to say, as you claim a debt from me,
That Aphrodite was my protectress on that voyage,
The goddess, her alone and no one else.
You're good with words, Medea. Perhaps it seems
Unchivalrous to suggest that it was simply Love   530
Whose arrows forced you to save my life.
I don't want to make an issue of it.
The assistance you gave was quite valuable.
But you did get better than you gave,
I think it's fair to say.
To begin with, instead of that uncivilised place,
You now live in Greece, a seat of justice
And the rule of law instead of mindless violence.
Everyone in Greece knows how clever you are.
You're famous. If you'd still been living   540
At the back of beyond, no one would have heard of you.

For my part, a house crammed full with gold,
Or the skill to sing and play like Orpheus,[13]
Would have no meaning without the fame.
I've spoken so far of my own achievements
But you did initiate this debate.
As for my marriage, my royal marriage,
That was a clever decision, you must agree,
As well as a sensible one, the best thing really
550   For you and the boys. No, just wait a moment.
When I arrived here from Iolcos,
Weighed down by a series of disasters,
What greater ambition could I have had,
As an immigrant, than to marry the king's daughter?
It was not – and I know this is what upsets you –
That I'd stopped loving you and fancied some
New woman or wanted a bigger family.
The boys. They're fine. No complaints there.
But so we could live a respectable life –
That's what it all comes down to –
560   And never go short. Oh, I know what it's like
For a man who's poor. Friends shun him,
This way I could have another family,
As befits my station, and bring them up as brothers
For our boys, one big happy family.
You don't need any more children, but for me
More sons would be a benefit to the others. Do you see?
What's wrong with that? But for your sexual jealousy.
You women. You're fixated.[14] You've convinced yourselves,
570   If you're happy in bed, nothing else matters.
If you're not, then everything's a disaster.
I wish there were some other way to father children.
No women.[15] That would solve everything.
CHORUS. A pretty speech, Jason.
But hardly fair on your wife, I think.
MEDEA. I may be alone in this – I usually am.
580   But for me he's a double-dyed villain
Who cloaks his weasel-words in sophistry.
A tongue so glib and devious

Will know no boundaries. Too clever by half.
You can drop the rhetoric.
One word will be enough.
If any of this were true, you'd have talked to me
Before this marriage, not kept it all a secret.

JASON. And so I would but for your attitude.
Mention the word marriage and look at you.
You can't control your fury.   590

MEDEA. That's not it, is it? As time went on
You found it inconvenient to have a foreign wife.

JASON. You know perfectly well, it's nothing about the princess
That made me want a royal marriage.
I've told you already, I did it for you,
To protect you and to father some royal sons,
Half-brothers for ours. For security.

MEDEA. I can do without that sort of security.
You can't buy peace of mind.

JASON. That attitude will get you nowhere.   600
Learn to be pragmatic.
Ride your good luck. Don't disparage it.

MEDEA. Don't insult my intelligence.
My departure lets you off the hook.

JASON. Have it your own way. You've only yourself to blame.

MEDEA. My marriage? My betrayal? What am I meant to have
                                                        done?

JASON. Curse the royal family. That's what you have done.

MEDEA. Not only the royal family.

JASON. I can't talk to you.
If you want it, for the children or yourself,   610
If you want it, there's money.
Just say the word. I'm quite prepared
To help you get by. I've friends. Abroad.
It's a genuine offer. You'd be a fool to turn it down.
Control that temper of yours and you'll be fine.

MEDEA. References! To friends of yours!
No thank you. I won't be needing them.
'Beware Greeks . . .', as they say.[16]

JASON. Oh for god's sake. I swear to you.

620   You, the boys, I only want to help.
             You don't know when you're well off, never have.
             That's your problem. You are so stubborn.
             All right. Spurn your friends. But on your head be it.
        MEDEA. Just go away, Jason! Your little bride's expecting you.
             You don't want to keep her waiting.
             Exit JASON.
             Go on. Go and get married. With luck,
             It won't be the wedding-day you have in mind.
        CHORUS. Passion. Too much passion.
             No merit in that,
             No reputation there.
630   Love, gentle love,
             Is a gift of the gods.
             I'll settle for that,
             With no searing, no poison,
             No obsession, no pain.

             Control. Moderation.
             I'll pray for them,
             I'll be comfortable with them.
             God preserve me
             From that madness,
640   The affliction that is sex,
             Without rhyme, without reason.
             Affection, but not passion.

             This is my home,
             My country, my place.
             May I never lose it,
             Never stray from security.
             Nothing worse, more pitiful.
             Rather death. Death rather,
650   Than a life with no country,
             No home. Nowhere.

             We know from experience.
             We see for ourselves,
             No city for you,
             No friend to take pity.

That's suffering at its worst.
God's curse on the man   660
Who closes his mind
To the helpless. I hate him.
Enter AEGEUS.

AEGEUS. Medea. It's good to see you.
  The warmest greetings I can offer to a friend.
MEDEA. And good to see you too, Aegeus.
  You're welcome. What are you doing here?
AEGEUS. On my way home from the oracle.
MEDEA. The oracle? What did you want at Delphi?[17]
AEGEUS. I'm childless. I wanted advice.
MEDEA. No family? God, no family?   670
AEGEUS. No family, no. Just bad luck, I suppose.
MEDEA. You are married? It's not, well, you know . . .
AEGEUS. Yes. I am married. We are married.
MEDEA. So, what did the oracle say?
AEGEUS. Excellent advice. I'm not sure quite what it means.
MEDEA. Can you tell me? The oracle? Would it be allowed?
AEGEUS. Oh, yes. It needs someone clever. Someone like you.
MEDEA. So? What did he say?
AEGEUS. He said 'Free not the wineskin's dangling foot.'
MEDEA. Till what? Till when?   680
AEGEUS. Till I get back home.
MEDEA. Oh. So, what are you doing here?
AEGEUS. There's someone called Pittheus – king of Troezen.[18]
MEDEA. A god-fearing man, they say.
AEGEUS. I thought I'd tell him. Tell him the oracle.
MEDEA. A good man. He'll sort it out for you.
AEGEUS. The best. We've fought together. Side by side.
MEDEA. Well, good luck. I hope it works.
AEGEUS. You look troubled, a bit out of sorts. Anything the
                                                  matter?
MEDEA. That husband of mine, Aegeus. What a swine.   690
AEGEUS. What do you mean? You're upset. I can see that.
MEDEA. He's wronged me and it's not my fault.
AEGEUS. Why, what on earth has he done? Tell me.
MEDEA. He's got himself a new wife.

AEGEUS. How dare he!

MEDEA. And I, his former lover, I'm humiliated.

AEGEUS. Did he fall in love with someone? Or fall out of love with
you?

MEDEA. He's in love, all right, and to hell with his family.

AEGEUS. Good riddance, if he's that bad.

700 MEDEA. It's the palace he's in love with.

AEGEUS. I don't quite follow. Who's her father?

MEDEA. Creon, the king. Creon.

AEGEUS. Now I see why you're upset.

MEDEA. I'm done for. They've exiled me.

AEGEUS. This is monstrous. Who has?

MEDEA. Creon has. He's thrown me out of Corinth.

AEGEUS. And Jason let him? That's unacceptable.

MEDEA. He says he fought it, but he's coping.
But I beseech, I beg you

710 By your head and by your knees,
Have pity. Pity me in my misery.
Don't see me left destitute.
Let me into your country and your home,
And love and good fortune will solve your problem,
Grant you children and peace at the last.
You don't realise what a stroke of luck you've had.
I can cure your childlessness.
I can make you a father. I know the remedy.

AEGEUS. For several reasons, madam, I'm inclined

720 To grant you what you ask. For the gods,
And for the children that you promise me,
Without whom Aegeus' name dies with him.
So be it. Come to Athens and in good faith
I'll do my best to see that you're safe.
One thing only, I'll not help you leave.
But find your way to where I live
And I can guarantee your safety.
But you must secure your own departure.

730 I want no trouble with strangers.

MEDEA. Fine. I'd like you to swear to that.

AEGEUS. You don't trust me? What's the matter?

MEDEA. I do trust you. But I have enemies.
  Creon and the house of Pelias.
  An oath cements my sanctuary.
  Your unsupported word, friend as you are,
  Without divine sanction, could be vulnerable
  Faced with a proclamation. I am powerless.
  They have money and a kingdom.   740
AEGEUS. You're looking ahead. That's good.
  If this is what you want, very well.
  Safest for me too, I think,
  To have a pretext for your enemies.
  Better for you too. Name your gods.
MEDEA. Swear by Mother Earth and by the Sun,
  My grandfather, and the whole pantheon.[19]
AEGEUS. What am I swearing to do? Tell me.
MEDEA. Swear you will never send me from your country.
  Swear, whatever enemy demands,   750
  While you live, you'll never give me up.
AEGEUS. I swear. By the Earth, by the Sun,
  By all the gods, I swear to do as you require.
MEDEA. That's good. On pain of what?
AEGEUS. Whatever perjurers suffer.
MEDEA. Goodbye then. Be happy. Everything's going to be fine.
  I'll make for your city as soon as I can.
  There's something I have to do first.
CHORUS. May Hermes, the escort, protect you, Aegeus,[20]
  Heading for home and the heart's desire   760
  That your generous spirit deserves.
  Exit AEGEUS.
MEDEA. Now Zeus, now Justice, daughter of Zeus,[21]
  Now light of the Sun, triumph, sisters,
  Triumph over the enemy. We're under way.
  Now we have the luxury of hope.
  An escape route. That was my weakness.
  Then who turns up? He does, my port in the storm.
  He's where I'll tie my tow-rope,   770
  Heading for a home in Athens.
  Let me explain all I have in mind,

Not the most cheerful of listening.
I will send a servant for Jason
And ask him to come to see me.
When he comes I will be very conciliatory,
Telling him how right he is, I now realise.
His royal marriage is a good thing all round,
Even if it means betraying me.
780 I'll ask for the children to remain here.
I don't want them left here, of course,
For my enemies to degrade,
But as instruments in killing the princess.
I'll send them with gifts,
Bridal gifts, to ask for an amnesty.
Gifts of a delicate dress and a gold tiara.
And if she puts them on, they'll kill her.
And they'll kill anyone who touches her,
Because I'll saturate my gifts with poison.
790 When that is done, it's done.
But what comes next, ah, there are the tears.
I have to kill the children. My children.
No one shall take them from me.
When Jason's world's destroyed,
Then I'll leave this land, depart,
Pursued by the most unnatural of crimes,
My murder of my children.
Sisters, I will not be mocked.
This has to happen. What is life for me?
No country. No home. No escape.
800 My fatal mistake was the day
I left my father's house, seduced by this Greek
And his fine words – god make him pay.
He'll never see alive the boys I bore,
Nor father a son on this brand-new wife
Condemned to die from my doctoring.
No weak little woman, here, no doormat.
Let nobody think it. Oh, no.
A good friend, but what an enemy.
810 Famous for it. That's Medea!

CHORUS. You've let me share your mind. I'm on your side.
  You know that. But there are laws. We're human.
  Medea, you can't do this.
MEDEA. There's no alternative. Say what you like.
  It's easy for you. What do you know of suffering?
CHORUS. Kill the boys? You'd bring yourself to do that?
MEDEA. He'll feel it.
CHORUS. And what about you? What does that make you?
MEDEA. What I am. Defeated. No point in your protesting.
                                                    Nurse,

Enter NURSE.
  Fetch Jason.   820
  You've always been someone I could trust.
  Tell no one. Nothing to anyone, if you care for me.
  No. Not that. As you are a woman.
  Exit NURSE.
CHORUS. Athenians, sons of Erechtheus,
  Children of the gods, are blessed.[22]
  In a holy land, clothed in peace,
  Nourished by judgement,
  Such air they breathe   830
  That there, long ago they say,
  The Nine, the Pierian Muses,
  Gave birth to Harmony, golden Harmony.[23]

  They tell too of Aphrodite,
  By the chuckling river Cephisus,[24]
  A breeze on her breath,
  A soft caress, no more,
  With roses in her hair,   840
  Offering love to the land,
  Love, tempered by moderation,
  Twin virtue with modesty.

  A city like that,
  A city of sacred rivers,
  Protector of travellers,
  To welcome an unholy child-killer?   850
  Murder. Look at it.

Look at it. Murder of your children.
Think again, I beg you.
Not killing your own children.

Where do you find the resolve,
The cast of mind, of heart,
To raise a hand against children,
Your own children?
860 Can you stare with steely eye
At those boys, your boys,
On their knees for their lives,
And lift your bloody hand?

Enter JASON followed by the NURSE.

JASON. You wanted to see me? Here I am.
I'm aware what you think of me, but, give me credit,
If you've something new to say, I'll listen.

MEDEA. Oh Jason, I'm sorry. Forgive me
870 For what I said. I was angry –
You know me. We were in love once.
I'm so furious with myself.
'What a fool you are, Medea,' I tell myself,
'To get upset with those who want to help,
Fighting the authorities, never mind your husband
Who only wants to do what's best for you,
Marrying a princess so my boys can have some brothers.
Control that temper of yours. You don't know
When you're well off, that's your problem.
There's the children, of course, but we're friendless,
880 On our own, living here on charity.'
So. I realise what a fool I've been,
Getting all upset. No point, is there?
In fact I have to thank you.
You did the sensible thing. I've been silly.
I should have been offering advice,
Giving a hand, making the new bed,
Happy to be your new wife's chamber-maid.
But, that's women for you. You know what we're like.
890 Don't pay us back in our own kind. Please.
Don't pay back foolishness with foolishness.

I give in. I've been very stupid.
But I'm better now.
Children. Children. Come out here a moment.
Hurry. Out here. Your father's here.
Come and see your father. And say goodbye.
Enter CHILDREN *with the* TUTOR.
We have to go. But no hard feelings.
We've made peace, your father and I.
We're friends again. Take his hand, then.
And the future? Well, who knows?   900
I'd rather not think about it. Oh children,
Your whole lives stretching out before you . . .
I'm frightened. I can't stop crying today.
There now. Quarrel's over with your father.
I can't see. I'm crying again.
CHORUS. And so am I. And so am I.
Please god, let things get no worse than this.
JASON. That's my girl. I don't blame you.
A woman's likely to get a bit emotional
With her husband marrying again.   910
Now you're making sense. Better late than never
But you can see the way the wind blows.
This is a reasonable woman talking.
You see, boys? Your father's had his thinking cap on.
God willing, he's sorted out your future for you.
You'll turn out to be big men, I think,
As big as your brothers in Corinth.
You keep growing, eh? And leave the rest
To your dad and any friendly god.
Fine lads you'll be when you're grown,   920
I reckon, ready to sort out my enemies for me.
Medea. Medea, why the tears?
You look as though you've seen a ghost.
I thought what I said would please you.
MEDEA. Nothing. It's nothing. I worry about them.
JASON. Come on. Cheer up. It'll work out fine.
MEDEA. You're right. Of course, you're right.
Us women. Always something to cry about.

JASON. But why are you worried about them?

930　MEDEA. I'm their mother aren't I? You talked about their future.
　　　　I just felt an ache. About the future.
　　　　Well, that is part of it. Why I asked you to come.
　　　　Let me tell you the rest.
　　　　It suited Creon's purpose, so it would seem,
　　　　To exile me. And so it suits me too.
　　　　I wouldn't wish to be an embarrassment
　　　　To you or to the palace, who seem to find me a threat.
　　　　So I'll take myself off, away from this land.
　　　　But so that the boys may be brought up by you,
940　　Please ask Creon not to banish them.

JASON. I don't hold out much hope but I'll try.

MEDEA. Then tell your wife. Tell your wife
　　　　To ask Creon not to banish them.

JASON. Very well. She'll agree to that.

MEDEA. She's a woman. She'll agree.
　　　　And I must do my part too.
　　　　I'll send her presents, a dress, finely woven,
　　　　And a gold coronet, gifts as beautiful
950　　As any you ever saw. The boys will take them.
　　　　Fetch them, one of you. Quick as you can.
　　　　Exit one of the CHILDREN.
　　　　A thousand blessings she shall win
　　　　With a man like you for a husband,
　　　　And decked out in finery my grandfather,
　　　　The Sun himself, handed down.
　　　　Enter CHILD with a box.
　　　　Here we are. Now boys, you must deliver these
　　　　Wedding presents to the princess, personally,
　　　　Into her hands. Special gifts.

JASON. Expensive presents. You are an idiot, Medea.
960　　They've plenty of dresses in the palace.
　　　　And gold. Keep them. Don't give them away.
　　　　She'll take more notice of what I tell her
　　　　Than of any presents, I'm sure of that.

MEDEA. Don't say that. Even a god likes a present.
　　　　Gold speaks louder than words – that's what they say –

Fortune favouring her, that's all.
She's young. She's a princess. To save my sons
From exile, never mind gold, I'd give my life.
Now listen, children. When you go into the grand house
Approach our young princess, my mistress,   970
And beg her, on your knees, not to banish you.
Give her the presents – most important that –
Into her hands. Give them to her yourselves.
Quick as you can. As soon as you've done it,
Come back here with good news for your mother.
Exeunt CHILDREN, TUTOR, NURSE *and* JASON.
CHORUS. Any hope that I cherished for the children's lives
    Snuffed out. Infanticide's abroad.
    The bride who says 'yes' to the gold-crusted crown,
    Says 'yes' to her death throes.
    She holds in her hands for her golden head   980
    A fatal decoration.

    So enchanting, so seductive, so divine.
    And the dress, like the crown.
    Just the things for a bride, Hell's bride.
    She'll be caught in the trap,
    Webbed in by the sticky strands of Death,
    Clinging, inexorable.

    And Jason, oh Jason, the ill-starred bridegroom,   990
    Son-in-law elect
    To the royal family, unwitting carrier
    Of death to your children,
    To your bride an agonising fate,
    Jason, what a downfall.

    And Medea, oh Medea, pity for you too,
    Mother and killer-elect
    Of your own children for vengeance.
    All over a new wife
    And a husband leaving against his oath   1000
    For some new bed.
    Enter TUTOR *and* CHILDREN.
TUTOR. Success, mistress. No exile for the boys.

The princess accepted the gifts
And has made peace with your children.
What's the matter?
Why are you looking like that?
It's good news isn't it? Why turn away?
You should be delighted. Isn't this what you wanted?

MEDEA. No, oh no.

TUTOR. This is a strange reaction. My news is good news.

MEDEA. No. No. No.

1010 TUTOR. What did I say? I thought the news was good.

MEDEA. Your news was news. Not your fault.

TUTOR. Then why are you looking like that? Why the tears?

MEDEA. 'The infernal machine', old man. I've set in train
Something fearsome, I and the gods.

TUTOR. Don't worry. The children will fetch you home in time.

MEDEA. I'll fetch home others first.

TUTOR. You're not the only one to be parted from your children.
You have to grin and bear it. People do.

MEDEA. Then so must I. Off you go indoors, now,

1020 And get the children ready for the day.
Exit TUTOR.
Oh my boys, my boys. This is your city,
Your home where I must leave you motherless.
Poor me.
I leave for somewhere else, a refugee,
Without the joy of watching you grow up,
Of seeing your prosperity, wives, weddings,
Wedding-torches, wedding-beds.
Selfishness, I suppose. It seems so pointless.
Why did I ever cherish you?

1030 Why bear you at all?
Difficult labours. Painful births.
You have these hopes – I did, poor fool that I was –
Of growing old pampered,
With loving care to help you from this life.
It's everyone's ambition. All gone.
A lovely dream. Without you
I'll live out my time fretting, embittered.

You'll never set eyes on your mother,
Never again. You'll have moved on.
No, don't. Don't look at me like that.   1040
Is that a smile? Will you ever smile again?
What am I to do? They melt my heart.
Dear friends, when I look at their faces,
My willpower deserts me. I can't do it.
Change of plan. I'll take them away.
What point in racking their father's heart
If I break my own twice over?
No. Never. Change of plan.
And yet . . . What's the matter with me?
They'd laugh at me, my enemies, for going soft.   1050
Coward. Coward, I must be strong.
No weakening. No relenting.
Children. Indoors.
Exeunt CHILDREN.
Now. Any of you who does not share my mind,
Go about your business. My hand will not weaken.
No. No, you can't. Medea, you can't go through with this.
You poor fool, let your children go.
They'll live on with you. Be happy.
No. Never. By all the hounds of hell,
I'll not hand over children of mine   1060
For my enemies to scorn and spit upon.
They have to die. And if that's going to happen,
I bore them so I have to do the killing.
All settled. There's no escape.
The coronet's on her head. The bride princess.
I know it. The dress is destroying her.
And I am starting on a terrible journey,
Terrible for my children too.
I have to speak to them.
Children, come here. Come here,
Re-enter CHILDREN.
Give me your hands.   1070
Beautiful hands. Lovely faces.
I love you. Wish you well. But not here.

Your father appropriated 'here'.
A kiss. A hug.
Such sweet breath children have.[25] Soft skin.
Off you go now. Go away!
Exeunt CHILDREN.
I can't look at you and do this.
No. Passion drowns my judgement,
1080   Passion the destructive force.
    CHORUS. A woman shouldn't probe
        The fine subtleties of myth,
        Or the struggle for survival.
        But I have. Often.
        We share a sense, we women,
        To help us understand.
        An instinct. Some of us.
        Only a few, perhaps, but some,
        Not incapable of reflection.

1090   And I say this. Those who miss out
        On experience.
        Who never have children,
        They're the lucky ones.
        They never know, the childless –
        They never have the chance –
        What a child may bring,
        Joy or grief, grief or joy.
        The childless never see
        That first sweet enchantment
1100   Shrivel, with time, into despair.

        How to bring them up.
        How to have something to leave them.
        Will they turn out frivolous?
        Will they turn out decent?
        There's no predicting; and no end to it.
        But worst, the worst
        Of any human experience.
        You become prosperous: they grow –
        Good children, fine young people –

And then some accident . . .   1110
Death steals them away,
Spirits them underground.
How does anyone survive that?
Why make yourself vulnerable,
Mortals to be toyed with by gods?
MEDEA. Sisters, I've lived a long time
   Under that sentence.
   Look. Someone coming.
   Jason's man, in a hurry, out of breath.
   Must be momentous news.   1120
   Enter MESSENGER.
MESSENGER. Terrible. Medea.
   You have done something terrible, unnatural.
   You have to go. Escape. Go.
   By ship. On land. Any way you can.
MEDEA. What on earth could require such a flight?
MESSENGER. The royal princess is dead.
   Creon too, victims of your venom.
MEDEA. Yes. I like the sound of this.
   You do me good. My friend for life.
MESSENGER. What are you saying? Woman, you're mad.
   You hear the royal house disintegrates   1130
   And you're pleased? Have you no fear?
MEDEA. I choose to see things in a different light.
   But, please, don't be in such a rush.
   Tell us about their deaths. And the more they suffered,
   I can assure you, my friend, the happier you'll make me.
MESSENGER. When the children, those two boys of yours,[26]
   Arrived with their father at the palace,
   They found it all decorated for the wedding,
   And us servants, who used to take your side,
   We were delighted. Word had got around, you see,
   That you and your husband had been reconciled.   1140
   People shook the boys' hands or patted their golden hair.
   I was so excited I followed them to the women's rooms.
   The Princess – she has our allegiance now, not you –
   She turned her gaze on Jason lovingly

Until she caught sight of the two children,
Then turned away and wouldn't look at them,
White as a sheet, furious to find them there.
1150   Your husband tried to placate her, saying,
'Don't be angry. Look. They only want to love you.
Your husband's friends must be your friends too.
They've brought presents. Accept them.
And ask your father to reprieve them. For me?'
The moment she saw the finery, she couldn't resist,
And gave in to all he asked.
Father and sons were barely out the door
Before she snatched the gorgeous dress and put it on,
1160   Then the gold coronet, checking in the mirror,
Giggling at the reflection of herself
As she arranged her curls round the tiara.
Then up she jumped from her dressing-table
And prinked around the room on her little white feet,
Glorying in her presents, again and again,
Posing, checking from head to heel.
Then, all of a sudden, something dreadful.
She changed colour, staggered,
Started to shiver, managed, just,
1170   To fall on the bed, not on the floor.
An old servant mumbled a prayer,
Assuming some god-frenzy or a fit.
But one look at her mouth –
Froth was bubbling from her lips,
Eyes rolling, colour drained.
No prayer then but a howl.
Someone ran for her father,
Someone else for the new husband,
1180   To tell them what was happening to the bride,
The corridors echoing with running feet.
For the time it takes a runner to complete a lap
She lay mute, poor woman,
Then started up, eyes tight shut, with a scream,
Ravaged by a double torture.
From the golden crown about her hair,

Flames shot, burning, ghastly.
But on her body so soft, the soft dress
That the children had brought began to feed.
She rose, ran, on fire,   1190
Tossing her head every way,
To shake off that halo. But it clung.
The more she shook, the more it flared.
Seared to the bone, at last she fell to the ground.
A father might recognise her, only a father.
You couldn't pick out her eyes,
Her features. Just blood dripping
From her head on to the flickering flames.
While her flesh, gorged on by the poison,   1200
Dribbled off her like gum from a pine.
Horrible. I can see it. No one dared touch her.
We were witnesses. We'd learned.
But her poor father knew nothing of this.
Rushing in he threw himself on her body,
Weeping, clinging to her, crying
'Child, poor child, who or what has destroyed you?
Who's turned this old man into a gravestone?
Oh child, let me die too.'   1210
Eventually his sobbing began to subside
And he started to try to get up.
But as he'd clung to her, she clung to him,
Like ivy clings to the laurel.
So with her dress he began a ghastly wrestling-match.
As he scrabbled to get to his knees,
She seemed to reach and grab him.
He fought her off and the flesh stripped from his bones.
At last – it took time – the wretched man
Succumbed to his fate and gave up the ghost.
The corpses lie together, child and father, close.   1220
'Let me die too.' The release of tears he craved.

And your part in this? I've said nothing.
You'll have secured your own escape.
'Walking shadows', that's all we are.
And so-called clever men, the silver-tongued –

I'm not afraid to admit it – pay too. They pay.
Call no man happy. That's what I say.
You might be luckier than your neighbour,

1230   Be more prosperous. But happy? Never.[27]

CHORUS. Disaster on disaster heaped on Jason,
       All in a single day. And he deserved it.
       But for you we do feel pity, poor daughter of Creon,
       Victim of Jason's wedding-plans.

MEDEA. Sisters, the die is cast. No delays.
       I must kill the children and make my escape.
       No delays, for them to fall into the clutches
       Of some other bloody, vengeful hand.

1240   They have to die, of course. So.
       I gave them life. I'll take it away again.
       Steel yourself, my heart. Why wait?
       Awful, but this you have to do.
       Grasp the sword, vile hand. Grasp it.
       The slow, short walk. To a life-sentence.
       Don't weaken. Don't think of them as children,
       Your children. Ignore love. For one short day
       Make believe they're not your boys.
       Then, then will be the time for grief.

1250   You kill them. Poor Medea. But I love them.
       Exit MEDEA.

CHORUS. Come Earth, look up,
       See, bright-shining Sun,
       This destructive, lethal woman,
       Planning infanticide.
       She's family, your family,
       God-blood
       Under threat from men. Stop her,
       Hold her back. God-born light of the Sun,
       A bloody, vengeful Fury is abroad.[28]

1260   Drive her out.

       Labour a waste.
       Nurturing a waste.
       Medea who left behind the threatening,
       Blue-black rocks,[29]

What fatal passion drives her,
Irredeemable,
To contemplate this murder?
Murder in the family for mortals
Means pollution. The Earth demands
A retribution and the gods comply.   1270

FIRST CHILD (*off*). Help!
    [*Iô moi.*]

CHORUS. Shouting. That's the children, surely?
    That woman, damnable woman.

FIRST CHILD (*off*). Help! Away from mother. How?
    [*Oimoi, ti drasô? Poi phugô mētros cheras?*]

SECOND CHILD (*off*). Don't know. Brother! Done for.
    [*Ouk oid', adelphe philtat'; ollumestha gar.*]

CHORUS. Should I go in? Someone should save them,
    The children.

FIRST CHILD (*off*). Help us! For god's sake, help!
    [*Nai, pros theôn arēxat'; en deonti gar.*]

SECOND CHILD (*off*). Sword. Can't escape. The sword . . .
    [*Hôs engus ēdē g'esmen arkuôn xiphous.*]

CHORUS. She's made of stone. Of iron, damn her,
    A woman who bears children   1280
    Only, herself, to kill them.
    I've heard of one, just one,
    In the past who cut down her own children,
    Ino, driven insane[30]
    When Hera harried her from home.
    She killed her two children, then herself.
    Poor creature, she went into the sea.
    Drowned herself from guilt.
    Can you imagine anything worse?   1290
    Sex. Passion.
    The trouble it brings.
    Enter JASON.

JASON. You, women. What are you hanging about here for?
    Is she in there? You know what she's done.
    Medea, is she there? Or has she got away?
    She'll have to tunnel her way out this time,

Or sprout wings and fly,
If she wants to avoid justice from the palace.
Killing the royal family!

1300 Does she think she'll get away with this?
It's the boys I'm worried about, not her.
She'll be paid back, eye for an eye,
But I mean to save my boys.
I don't want the family taking it out on them
For what that damned mother of theirs has done.

CHORUS. Oh Jason. Poor Jason. You don't know the half of it
Or you could never have spoken as you have.

JASON. Meaning? Is she going to kill me now?

CHORUS. Your sons. They're dead. Their mother killed them.

1310 JASON. What? Finished. Destroyed.

CHORUS. It's your children who are finished. Think of them.

JASON. She killed them. Where? Out here? Inside?

CHORUS. Open the doors to see the carnage.

JASON. Break in. Force your way in.
I'll see this double horror,
Both boys dead. And the woman I mean to kill.

Enter MEDEA *above.*

MEDEA. Why this assault on the doors,
Looking for the bodies and their killer?
No need. Anything you want to say,

1320 Say it. You cannot touch me now.
My grandfather, the Sun, has furnished me
With a chariot to protect me from my enemies.

JASON. You plague. You hateful thing. You woman
Detested by god, by me, by every mortal man.
You dared to draw a sword and plunge it
Into children, your children, my children.
You do this and can still look at the sun
And at the earth. No crime's more monstrous.
My curse, till death. Now at last I see you as you are.

1330 I never realised when I brought you to Greece
From your home, that primitive country,
You were a traitress to your father and your land.
A degenerate. Now the gods heap retribution

On me for your slaughtering your own brother
Before you ever embarked on the good ship *Argo*.
That was only the start. We married.
You had my children. Now you've killed them.
Why? Sex, just for the sake of sex.
No Greek woman would have done it.
Yet instead of one of them I deigned to marry you.   1340
What a wife you turned out to be.
An animal, not a woman,
A savage, some prehistoric monster.
Nothing I can say would touch your sort.
Your heart's too hard.
Vile. Leave, then, drenched in your children's blood.
Leave me to grieve my fate.
No new marriage to enjoy.
Never again to speak to the boys I fathered
And brought up. A beaten man.   1350

MEDEA. We could debate at some length about this,
I think, but there's no real point.
Zeus knows how you've been treated and what I did.
I deserved better than contempt for my bed,
Rejection for something tastier. Oh, no.
You mocked me, Jason. While that brand-new bride
And her father Creon wanted me out of here.
'Animal', am I? 'Not a woman.'
'Savage. Prehistoric monster.'
That's what it took to crush your heart.   1360

JASON. Oh, you suffer too, do you, like me?

MEDEA. Suffer, yes. You cannot mock me. That's my consolation.

JASON. What a mother, children! What an evil woman!

MEDEA. What a father, boys! Victims of that male disorder.

JASON. It wasn't my hand killed them.

MEDEA. Conceit, rather, and a second marriage.

JASON. And that's worth an execution?

MEDEA. It's just a peccadillo, is it?

JASON. To a proper wife, yes. To you everything's wrong.

MEDEA. They're dead now. I hope it hurts.   1370

JASON. They'll live on in my vengeance, never fear.

MEDEA. The gods recognise who started this.

JASON. They recognise a warped mind, that's for sure.

MEDEA. Detest me then. Twisted words and I reject them.

JASON. And I reject yours. I propose a truce.

MEDEA. On what terms? I'm agreeable.

JASON. Let me have the bodies to mourn and then to bury.

MEDEA. Oh no you don't. I'll bury them.[31]

    I'll take them to Hera's precinct

1380 To save their graves from desecration.

    But I will establish a ceremony here in Corinth

    With rites to atone for this bloody deed,

    While I go to Athens

    To live under the protection of Aegeus.

    But for you, the dirty death that you deserve,

    With your skull smashed under the *Argo*.[32]

    And the memory of that woman to your dying day.

JASON. If children are protected by a Fury,

1390 Let her and Justice consume you.

MEDEA. What power, what deity, do you think,

    Will listen to a condemned perjurer?

JASON. Child-killer!

MEDEA. Oh, go and bury your bride.

JASON. I'm going. A father, childless.

MEDEA. You don't know suffering. Wait till you're old.

JASON. Children . . .

MEDEA. My children, not yours.

JASON. Their murderer.

MEDEA. To torture you.

1400 JASON. Let me touch them. Kiss them. Just once.

MEDEA. Now you want to touch them. And kiss them, now.

    What about exile? It was a different story then.

JASON. Please. For god's sake,

    Grant me just one touch.

MEDEA. No. It's pointless to ask.

JASON. Do you hear how she rejects me?

    Do you hear, Zeus, when I've suffered

    At her savage, child-killer's hands?

    What's left for me, I'll do.

I'll mourn and call heaven to witness
That you killed my children
And would not let me bury them,
Or even touch their bodies.
Would they had never been born
To die cut down by you.
Exit JASON.

CHORUS. Olympian Zeus ordains,[33]
 The gods accomplish, strangely.
 Things rarely end as you expect.
 The unexpected is god's way,
 The lesson of this story.

Notes

1 l.1 *Argo*: the Nurse refers to the voyage of Jason and his men (the Argonauts) who sailed in the *Argo* to Colchis to bring back the Golden Fleece. Jason was told by his uncle Pelias, who has usurped the throne of Iolcos, that he would give up the throne if Jason would bring him the Golden Fleece. Long before, a winged ram with a golden fleece had helped Helle and Phrixus escape their stepmother Ino (mentioned later in the play) who was trying to kill them. Helle fell off the back of the ram in flight, and drowned: she gave her name to the Hellespont. Phrixus escaped to Colchis, where he sacrificed the ram, whose fleece was then guarded by a dragon. With the help of Medea, daughter of Aeetes, King of Colchis, Jason managed to pass all the tests set by her father, steal the Golden Fleece and return to Iolcos with Medea.

2 l.10 *daughters of Pelias*: Pelias had set Jason what he thought was an impossible task. When Jason returned and Pelias refused to give up the throne, Medea showed the daughters of Pelias how she could make an old ram young, by boiling it in a cauldron filled with magic herbs. It sprang out, a frisky young lamb. The daughters tried to restore their father Pelias in the same way, but Medea gave them different herbs. The result was a dead Pelias, killed by his own daughters. Acastus, Pelias' son, banished his guilty sisters, together with Medea and Jason.

3 l.69 *dominoes*: the game *pessoi*. The term can indicate dice, draughts, or checkers, here translated 'dominoes'.

4 ll.96–213: this is a lyric *kommos* or lamentation: an exchange in a lyric metre by a character (here, the Nurse and Medea offstage) with the Chorus. The usual metre of dialogue is iambic. The varied metres of lyric passages like this one often convey heightened emotion.

5 l.160 *Goddess of justice, goddess of childbirth*: Medea calls on Themis, the goddess of justice, and Artemis, the goddess of childbirth, who can also protect women and carry out vengeance.

6 l.168 *father . . . brother*: Medea invokes her father Aeetes and her home, Colchis, and refers to her brother Apsyrtus, whom she killed and dismembered, scattering the pieces of his body to delay her father in his pursuit (he had to gather up the pieces for burial).

7 l.222 *If you're a foreigner, well, it's best to conform*: Euripides talked frequently about exile, and died in Thessaly himself. In the *Phoenissae* there is a dialogue between Polyneices and his mother Jocasta. She asks what is difficult for exiles. And Polyneices answers that the worst is not having free speech (ll.390–1). He uses the word *parrhesia*, the freedom of speech that citizens in a democracy enjoy.

8 l.284 *daughter*: Creon's daughter is called Glaukē in the hypothesis, or story of the play, which dates from about the first century AD. Later writers call her Creusa. Various sources tell us that the children's names are Mermeros and Pheres.

9 l.286 *clever*: Medea says that children should not be taught to be clever. 'Ignorance is bliss' is a frequent theme in Euripides. The *Bacchae* is a good source of examples,

from the phrase 'learning is not wisdom' (*to sophon d'ou sophia*, l.395), to Cadmus telling his daughter Agave that if she remains in ignorance throughout her life, she could have a semblance of happiness (ll.1261–2). Euripides probably suffered himself for being too clever for his own good. He won only four dramatic victories in his lifetime, compared with Aeschylus' thirteen and Sophocles' twenty-four.

10 l.394 *Hecate*: a goddess who governed sorcery and was associated with Hades. She is also closely linked to Artemis. Circe, the primal witch, is Medea's aunt, and Hecate is sometimes considered Circe's mother. Hecate is often in Medea's genealogical chart.

11 l.407 *granddaughter of the Sun*: Medea's grandfather is Helios the Sun who will send her a dragon-drawn chariot so that she can escape at the end of the play.

12 l.476 *I saved your life*: Medea tells Jason that he was able to accomplish the tasks set him by Aeetes only through her help. The tasks were yoking the fire-breathing bulls and sowing the deadly field. When Aeetes still refused to give him the Golden Fleece, Jason then had to slay the sleepless dragon of the many coils who guarded it. That is all that Euripides tells us. It is significant that Medea here does not bring up killing her brother Apsyrtus. From Apollonius Rhodius' *Argonautica* (third century BC) we learn that Medea gave Jason an ointment to cover himself and his weapons. By this means he was able to yoke the fire-breathing bulls and plough a field in which he sowed dragon's teeth. Medea told him how to overcome the fighting men who sprang up from the dragon teeth: he threw a boulder into their midst and they slew each other. Then Medea lulled the vigilant dragon with charms and

smeared ointment on its eyes so it would sleep. This enabled Jason to steal the fleece.

13 l.543 *Orpheus*: son of the god Apollo and famous for his music and poetry.

14 l.569 *You're fixated*: Jason's accusation that Medea and all women are obsessed with sex has become a misogynist commonplace and often used as an excuse for controlling women: cf. Byron, 'Man's love is of man's life a thing apart,/'Tis women's whole existence' (*Don Juan*, Canto 1, st. 200). Aristophanes has women complain in the *Thesmophoriazousae* that Euripides has painted women as so mad for sex that they are always under suspicion (l.390 ff.). We are told that Hera blinded Tiresias when he told her that women had 90 per cent of the pleasure in love-making, whereas men only 10 per cent, and he based this on his experience of having spent years as both a woman and a man (see Ovid, *Metamorphoses*, III, ll.320–38).

15 l.572 *I wish . . . No women*: Jason's misogynist lines suggesting that man ought to get his children by means other than woman and thus avoid a major evil echo Hippolytus' wish that children could be purchased and thereby avoid women altogether (*Hippolytus*, ll.616–24). There have been comparable misogynist echoes throughout the ages from Milton's *Paradise Lost* (X, l.888 ff.), to Shakespeare's *King Lear*, IV, vi.

16 l.618 *'Beware Greeks'*: translator's licence; a reference forward to Virgil's *Timeo Danaos, et dona ferentes* (*Aeneid*, II, l.48): 'I fear Greeks, even if they bring gifts.'

17 l.667 *Delphi*: Medea asks Aegeus what he asked Apollo at Delphi, the site of the 'omphalos', the shrine known as 'the navel-stone' (so called because Zeus released two eagles from the eastern and western extremities of the

world and they met at Delphi, which was therefore considered the centre of the world). In the shrine there was a conical stone at which suppliants sat when they consulted the oracle. The pythoness, or oracle, sat on a holy tripod. This priestess was named after the python, sacred to Themis, whom Apollo slew when he took over Delphi and made it his seat of prophecy. Delphi figures prominently in many Greek tragedies, for instance, as the source of prophecy for Oedipus, and also the site of Neoptolemus' death in Euripides' *Andromache*. The answers the oracle gives are ambiguous, as here, 'Free not the wineskin's dangling foot, before you reach home' (l.679). This refers to Aegeus' sojourn at Troezen where he drank too much wine and slept (freed the wineskin's dangling foot) with Aethra, the daughter of Pittheus. She gave birth to Theseus, who was the source of Aegeus' death, because when Theseus returned home victoriously from Crete after slaying the Minotaur in the Cretan labyrinth, he did not change his sails from black to white to signal his victory. Aegeus in despair committed suicide. He dived into the sea and drowned: that sea is named after him, the Aegean. The oracle thus did not tell Aegeus how to get children, but rather how to avoid having a son who would be the source of his death. A comparable oracle was given to Laius, the father of Oedipus.

18 l.683 *Pittheus – king of Troezen*: when Pittheus heard the oracle, he arranged that his daughter Aethra would sleep with Aegeus. He wanted a son to rule Athens. He got his wish (see last note).

19 l.746 *Swear by Mother Earth . . . pantheon*: Medea has Aegeus swear by the Earth, and the Sun, her grandfather, and all the gods of heaven. She is invoking the elements:

Mother Earth and Father Sun.

20 1.759 *Hermes*: the Chorus appropriately ask that Hermes, the god of travellers, protect Aegeus on his trip home.

21 1.762 *Zeus*: Medea invokes Zeus, guardian of oaths, and Justice, who also stands by oaths, and the light of the Sun, who brings lies to light. They are potent allies against Jason.

22 1.824 *Athenians, sons of Erechtheus, children of the gods*: Erechtheus in early legend was identified with Erichthonius, the son of Hephaestus, god of fire, and Pallas Athena, goddess of wisdom, with Earth acting as the womb. Erechtheus was an early king of Athens and ancestor of the Athenians. The shrine called the Erechtheum was built on the Acropolis in Athens.

23 1.831 *Harmony*: Harmonia, the love-child of Aphrodite, goddess of love, and Ares, god of war (others say of Zeus and Electra), grandmother of Dionysus and Pentheus (see Euripides' *Bacchae*), was married to Cadmus, the founder of Thebes. Harmonia is here symbolically called the child of the Muses: the nine Muses (art) give birth to harmony. Pieria is where they lived, in Macedonia.

24 1.835 *Cephisus*: a god of the river, related to Erechtheus, and ancestor of the Athenians. Aphrodite is associated with the Muses and beauty (see Sophocles, *Oedipus at Colonus*, ll.691 ff., just after he mentions the river Cephisus). She had a temple near both the Cephisus and the river Ilissus. Aphrodite keeps the land fertile and covered with flowers, with the help of the rivers. The Chorus invokes the benevolent deities who encourage fertility and creation, in contrast with the destructive Medea. They ask her how she thinks such a people will welcome a woman who has killed her children. How can

such a holy place accept an unholy murderess?

25 l.1075 *Such sweet breath*: Medea comments on the sweet
breath and soft skin of her children; this parallels other
moments in plays by Euripides when a mother must say
goodbye to a child about to die. Cf. *Trojan Women*,
ll.757–8: 'Oh dearest child, nestling against your mother,
how sweet is your breath.' The suffering of the mother is
distilled into a physical description of the pleasure of
touching her child. Medea not only loves her own
children, but gradually realises how valuable a child is to
the father: Creon is concerned about his daughter; Jason
says he wants to provide for his sons; and Aegeus is
consulting oracles about how to get children. Medea sees
this is the best route for her vengeance: she not only
destroys Jason's own children, but any chance of having
them with his new bride.

26 ll.1136–1230: the Messenger speech regularly features in
most Greek tragedy, but it is a Euripidean speciality. It is
a *tour de force* for an actor who likes to tell stories.
Graphic language enhances the tale. Euripides indulges in
some of the most gruesome details describing the death of
the Princess and her father, particularly when he describes
the flesh falling off Glaukē like sap from a pine. There
were comparable descriptions in the *Hippolytus* and the
Bacchae: in the latter Pentheus' body had to be
reassembled for burial like pieces in a jigsaw puzzle.

27 l.1230 *happy? Never*: see McDonald, *Terms for Happiness
in Euripides*, pp. 55–6. This claim about happiness not
lasting is a variation on the commonplace: 'Call no man
happy before his death'. One must evaluate a person's
happiness only after one can see a man's entire life. This
saying is found in Herodotus, I, 32, 7; Aeschylus,

Agamemnon, ll.928–9; Sophocles, *Women of Trachis*, ll.1–3; *Oedipus Tyrannus*, ll.1528–30; *Tyndareus* and *Tyro* (both Nauck, frag. 588 and 601); and Euripides, *Children of Heracles*, ll.865–6; *Andromache*, ll.100–2; *Trojan Women*, ll.509–10; and *Iphigenia at Aulis*, ll.160–2 (a slight variation, but close to *Medea*, l.1230: no one is happy or free from sorrow throughout his life).

29 l.1259 *Fury*: the Chorus see the house subjected to avenging spirits, an Erinys or Fury, driven by an *alastor*, an avenging deity. Medea embodies vengeance. In Aeschylus, an Erinys (Helen and her 'marriage') came to Troy, similarly bringing disaster (*Agamemnon*, l.749). In Sophocles' *Electra*, Aegisthus and Clytemnestra were called a double Erinys (l.1080).

29 l.1264 *the threatening blue-black rocks*: Jason had to sail through the clashing rocks (also called the 'dark rocks'), the Symplegades, when he came to Colchis. After he was able to make his way past them, they became fixed. This feat is dramatically described by Apollonius Rhodius (*Argonautica*, 2, ll.549–606; see note 12). They released a dove, and when it made its way through with only its tail feathers lost, the men followed rowing furiously. Athena held the rocks apart, and pushed their boat through. Like the dove, the *Argo* lost only its stern ornament.

30 l.1284 *Ino*: Ino is compared to Medea. Hera, Zeus' lawful wife, drove Ino and her husband Athamas mad because Ino, Semele's sister, had been nurse to Dionysus, the son of Zeus and Semele. In her madness Ino killed one of her sons, Melicertes, by throwing him into boiling water, and Athamas stabbed the other, mistaking him for a deer. Ino jumped into the sea with Melicertes' body. She became Leucothea, the White Goddess. Together with her son,

now called Palaemon, she guided ships beset by storms. Jason's remark that no Greek woman would have done what Medea did (ll.1339–40) is ironic when Ino is given as a parallel. Procne offers another, having killed her son to avenge herself on her husband Itys for raping and mutilating her sister Philomela.

31 l.1378 *I'll bury them*: Medea says that she will bury the children in Hera's precinct so that their bodies will be protected; at the same time she will establish a ceremony. It is common for Euripides to speak of the establishment of some rite at the end of his plays (see *Hippolytus*, ll. 1423–30 and *Iphigeneia in Tauris*, ll.1449–61). A scholiast, or commentator on Euripides, tells us that Parmeniscus said that the people of Corinth slew Medea's children in the temple of Hera. To atone for this, noble children must serve each year in the temple (this custom did take place in historical times up to 146 BC, the destruction of Corinth by the Romans). By blaming the crime on Medea, Euripides could be accused of being unpatriotic, since he took the blame away from the Corinthians, who were hostile at this time (the beginning of the Peloponnesian War). The establishment of a ritual to commemorate Medea's children is perhaps a gesture by Euripides to the conventional myth.

32 l.1386 *With your skull smashed*: Medea prophesies how Jason will die: with his skull crushed by a rotting piece of the *Argo*, the ship that carried him to Colchis where he fought successfully and won the Golden Fleece. The ignominious end of this hero is typical of Euripides' deconstruction of conventional heroes. Denys Page tells us in his edition of the *Medea* that this piece of the *Argo* was probably hanging in a temple, a thank-offering after

Jason's successful voyage. It is appropriate for Jason, the
oath-breaker, to die in the temple of Hera, the patron
goddess of marriage.

33 l.1416 *Olympian Zeus ordains* . . .: similar lines conclude
the *Alcestis*, *Andromache*, *Helen* and *Bacchae*. They are
sometimes considered a signal to the audience for
applause. They commemorate the unexpected, as visited
by the gods on mankind, and a good playwright on his
audience.

Methuen Classical Greek Dramatists

Aeschylus Plays: One
(Persians, Seven Against Thebes, Suppliants,
Prometheus Bound)

Aeschylus Plays: Two
(Oresteia: Agamemnon, Libation-Bearers, Eumenides)

Aristophanes Plays: One
(Acharnians, Knights, Peace, Lysistrata)

Aristophanes Plays: Two
(Wasps, Clouds, Birds, Festival Time, Frogs)

Aristophanes & Menander: New Comedy
(Women in Power, Wealth, The Malcontent,
The Woman from Samos)

Euripides Plays: One
(Medea, The Phoenician Women, Bacchae)

Euripides Plays: Two
(Hecuba, The Women of Troy, Iphigeneia at Aulis,
Cyclops)

Euripides Plays: Three
(Alkestis, Helen, Ion)

Euripides Plays: Four
(Elektra, Orestes, Iphigeneia in Tauris)

Euripides Plays: Five
(Andromache, Herakles' Children, Herakles)

Euripides Plays: Six
(Hippolytos, Suppliants, Rhesos)

Sophocles Plays: One
(Oedipus the King, Oedipus at Colonus, Antigone)

Sophocles Plays: Two
(Ajax, Women of Trachis, Electra, Philoctetes)

Methuen Student Editions

Methuen World Classics
include

Jean Anouilh (two volumes)
Brendan Behan
Aphra Behn
Bertolt Brecht (seven volumes)
Büchner
Bulgakov
Calderón
Čapek
Anton Chekhov
Noël Coward (eight volumes)
Feydeau (two volumes)
Eduardo De Filippo
Max Frisch
John Galsworthy
Gogol
Gorky
Harley Granville Barker
    (two volumes)
Henrik Ibsen (six volumes)
Alfred Jarry
Lorca (three volumes)

Marivaux
Mustapha Matura
David Mercer (two volumes)
Arthur Miller (five volumes)
Molière
Musset
Peter Nichols (two volumes)
Clifford Odets
Joe Orton
A. W. Pinero
Luigi Pirandello
Terence Rattigan
    (two volumes)
W. Somerset Maugham
    (two volumes)
August Strindberg
    (three volumes)
J. M. Synge
Ramón del Valle-Inclán
Frank Wedekind
Oscar Wilde

For a Complete Catalogue of Methuen Drama titles
write to:

Methuen Drama
215 Vauxhall Bridge Road
London SW1V 1EJ

or you can visit our website at:

www.methuen.co.uk